Triumph through the Tears

Finding Hope and Purpose Through Loss

by Jessica Moyer

New Vibe Press

Your Story is Our Story

Your Story is Our Story!

dedication

This book is written and dedicated in memory of my loving sweet baby boy Steven. His presence taught me the true lessons in life.

*Take nothing for granted because
life is precious and fleeting.*

Love knows no boundaries.

*Faith will carry me through the darkest of times
and there is always a beacon of light out there.*

*Purpose will abound out of the most difficult
and unexpected journeys in life.*

table of contents

Foreword

Written by Jay, my loving supportive husband

We all have our own crosses to bear. My wife has had to deal with many negative emotional states in a very short window of her life. She has lived through a lifetime of grief in less than a decade. We all carry and manage grief in a different way. The decisions you make from your lowest point is what will shape your future. Jess chose the path that is difficult for many to choose: find Hope and Purpose through her many tears.

At some point in all of our lives we have to look in the mirror and face our challenges head on. This decision is not black or white, A or B or one versus two. Other factors always play a role in our decision making process. Crushing anxiety from the loss of a child, dealing with the death of a parent at too young of an age, caring for living and growing children, and the medical decision making and care of a parent post stroke create a reality that is foggy. Your window into your own soul and the image of yourself in the mirror fades, your time for self care dwindles and you have no time to solve all the additional problems that have been placed on your plate let alone your own problems.

Since I have known Jess for more than half my life, she has always invested in others before investing in herself. Parents, siblings, friends, family, children and spouse were always chosen above herself. But, as the haze of her decision making process began to lift in the early to mid 2010's she chose to pivot. The negative of putting others before self became an encouragement toward recovery.

She discovered that the classroom of her life had earned her the knowledge on how to manage grief. This positive spin on a negative attribute created a pathway that allowed her heart to begin to heal. Discovering the antidote to her grief started to turn the tide of negative emotions.

Dance is medicine. The decision to invest in a Zumba certification would plant the seeds of growth for her ascent out of the depths of her grief. This one day certification had a significant return on investment. It allowed her an outlet where she could create a community. This community of women also carried with them their own stories of grieving. This gave her the realization that she was not the only one that was bearing a cross. It gave her the awareness that her anguish could help others heal from their own stories of grief.

Her interaction with individuals in the community continued through fitness and her growth mindset created a business idea (Purposeful Life and Wellness Coach) that continued to heal/callus her own wounds and would lead to where she is today. Jess's soul is an open book. Her faith over fear mindset allows those that she coaches to operate in a judgment free zone.

Jess's journey is a voyage of dealing with the demons of what a broken heart can place upon your soul, cleansing from that crushing weight of grief and finding inner peace. This book will give you a map to create your own journey to rise from the ashes of your grieving process, give you the tools to move in a positive direction, wash away your sorrow and recreate your future. The seeds of growth are in each of us. Allow a seasoned gardener of hope, growth and healing from grief to lead you on a straightforward path!

Introduction

*"It is not what happens to you in life
that determines how far you will go,
but how you respond to what happens."*
-Zig Ziglar

As a young girl, my Father had always reminded me that nobody is guaranteed anything in life. Then he would follow up with- except these two things- paying taxes and death. I had read that this was once said by the famous inventor and one of the Founding Fathers, Benjamin Franklin, in 1789. It is a harsh reminder of the certainties of being human and living on this planet. In many ways, I felt naive to both of these topics, particularly because of a protected childhood. Little did I know how the reality and the sting of Death would forever affect my life.

Yes, the word death is gloomy and can be scary for some people. However, it is a fact that we all must face sooner or later that every living thing on this planet will perish. Many people fear death and try to avoid the topic at all costs. It is not a conversation that anyone prefers to discuss or bring up because it can create discomfort. Death is the physical end on Earth for the person we so dearly love. Their pain and suffering is gone. However what is left behind for all of the survivors is great heartache, extensive grief, and a true unraveling of the soul.

But death can also create a rebirth in our life. If we allow the pain to pass through us and work to find the purpose in the loss, the blessings and lessons the loved one left behind, then death can also lead to beautiful new beginnings. The tears we shed for the heart wrenching pain and loss can be replaced with tears of thanksgiving if you allow yourself to be open to new possibilities. Our tears can also lead us to triumph and victory in the unimaginable battles we may face.

Grief from loss or death has no consistent timeline or definite end. It comes and goes, it creeps up at the most unusual times and there is no right or wrong timeframe. Grief does not discriminate based on color, age, gender, religion or economic class. Grief can be caused by many things including but not limited to: loss of a person, pet, loss of identity from injury or sickness, loss of a job, loss of a relationship or marriage, or loss of a life you thought you were meant to have. No one can escape grief! Once you experience it, you will always have a cross to carry. It may feel lighter at times, but it is always present.

Loss forever impacts our life, but we have a CHOICE about how we LIVE the rest of our life. Life is short and we don't know when our time is up. Do you want to live the rest of your life with hopelessness or hope? As the scriptures say *"I know the plans I have for you,plans to prosper you and not harm you, plans to give you hope and a future."* - Jeremiah 29:11. Our God wants us to seek the light and make way for a hopeful future despite the trials and tolls of our days.

My desire in sharing my story is to inspire those who have suffered in the shadows from loss and death. My wish is to offer hope and encouragement that life will continue to be beautiful, but just in a different way and that you can use the "tools" that I found most useful from my own personal journey to build your world to one with hope, purpose and joy!

With this book I hope to encourage you to use your grief and sadness to propel your purpose. You are here for a reason. Let me lift you from your dark place and inspire you to live and love fully despite the heartache and sadness you've experienced and may continue to experience.

I will share my journey of loss to hope and how strangely the shower was where I worked through the grief and ultimately found a path to purpose, growth and triumph! Your "place" may be different but recognizing that we need a safe place, literally or figuratively, to work through our emotions and learn how to adapt to a new normal of hope and purpose is imperative.

I love the words of Brene Brown, best selling author and speaker on the topics of courage, empathy and vulnerability, "When we deny our stories, they define us. When we own our stories, we get to write the ending."

Never in my worst of nightmares could I have imagined the tremendous loss I would begin to experience at the young age of twenty eight. However, somehow and in some way God had a plan in bringing me through this overwhelming pain. I believe this purpose that I discovered was to share my personal story with you and to guide those in deep sorrow to find hope and purpose through their tears. Deep in my soul I knew this pilgrimage I was embarking on would lead to beautiful pages in my chronicle of life. We all have the free will to choose how the next pages of our existence will be written.

As Zig Ziglar, one of my mentors, states, "It is not what happens to you in life that determines how far you will go, but how you respond to what happens." If an ordinary curly haired 5 foot girl from a small town in New Jersey can survive, thrive and eventually celebrate triumph through tragedy and loss so can you.

Foreshadowing

I don't have the best memory, but you know how there are certain encounters in life that just stick with you? I vividly remember the day I was making a pharmaceutical call to a doctor's office in Berlin, New Jersey and I ran into a rep from another company. Sometimes these encounters with our competitors can be uncomfortable, but being a chatty, outgoing person I struck up a conversation with this man. I could see such sadness in his eyes and knew he had a troubling story behind him. I asked him if he was okay and he responded with something I wasn't prepared for. He told me his two-year-old son had recently passed from cancer, but he had to get back to work to keep his mind occupied. A flood of emotions came over me because as a mom to a 6-month-old baby, I couldn't even imagine the pain this young Dad was experiencing. I gave him a hug and offered him what felt like an inadequate, insincere "I am so sorry" comment. No one knows really what the right response is when someone shares this heartache. After I left, I was so troubled and disturbed wondering, how is this fair in life? I couldn't imagine ever having to bury my own flesh and blood. That chance encounter struck such an uneasy chord deep in my soul.

I continued in the pharmaceutical industry for another year until my husband, Jason, received his Doctorate of Optometry degree from the Pennsylvania College of Optometry. Upon graduation, he had to fulfill his active duty military obligation due to receiving an Army ROTC scholarship for his undergraduate degree. His first duty station following the Army Officer Basic Course at Fort Sam Houston, Texas was at Fort Meade, Maryland. I chose to leave my job and become a full-time stay-at-home mom. This was a dream of mine growing up! I was so excited to have more children, nourish my family and do all the fun mom stuff. However, life doesn't prepare you for the unexpected as a mother who loves her children.

In June of 2000, we settled into our new home in Columbia, Maryland. With great anticipation, we set out to start a new chapter in our lives in building our family. It wasn't long until I excitedly became pregnant with my second child and found out it was going to be a boy. Jay and I were thrilled that Isobel would soon have a baby brother! Our dreams were coming to fruition and we felt overwhelmingly blessed. Soon the joy of a new pregnancy was quickly replaced with endless hours and days of nausea, vomiting and sickness. The only place I seemed to get a feeling of relief was the shower.

This cubicle became my space to escape the constant waves of nausea and actually feel good for just a few minutes. The water felt so refreshing and took my mind away from the hormonal war raging inside my body as a result of pregnancy. Little did I know just how the shower would become a refuge for so much to come in my life.

The Shower Experience

As I turn the faucet on in the shower I prepare for the waves of emotions that will wash over me. I am not sure exactly when I realized that my "watering hole" known as the shower, a place to cleanse your body, became my vestibule for working through grief and finding my purpose. Maybe it was the day I was told my firstborn son would never live past the age of one? It could have been the day I had to say goodbye to my hero, my Father, who was being taken off of life support, or maybe even the day I hugged my husband goodbye for his deployment as I was nine months pregnant with my second son?

The shower became the only place where I felt safe to express my emotions. It was the only place that was truly private - no one could hear my sobs or see the anguish I felt as my body shook from the tears.

Did the shower really cleanse and wash away the sadness or was it me working through all of the thoughts racing in my brain like a fish swimming in a tiny bowl, with nowhere to escape? It didn't matter.

The truth is, this rectangular box became my safe haven. Just as life has peaks and valleys, through the years my showers have gone through patterns of heavy rain storms, gentle cleansing spring rains and eventually rainbows. I compare my showers to several different "boxes" in life depending on the scenario playing out in my brain. Please, bear with me as I explain.

Chapter 1

"You may be gone from my sight,
but you are never gone from my heart"
-Winnie the Pooh

September 25th, 2001

As I stepped into the warm shower, my body was ice cold. The news I had just received hours ago left me with both a numbness and pain I will feel forever. Thank God there was a seat in the shower to hold me up. How, in just minutes, could my world be rocked to the core? As I let the water hit me, I couldn't decipher the tears.

My pregnancy and labor with Steven seemed to go okay, yet from the week after his birth until that day, I knew deep in my heart something wasn't right. I couldn't compare the experience to the birth of my daughter because my firstborn, Isobel, was born at 31 weeks and spent the first month in the NICU or Neonatal intensive care unit (More on this later).

Steven seemed different though. He had a weak cry and his body movement seemed limited. He wasn't reaching even the simplest of milestones. He had trouble just holding a pacifier in his mouth. His arm and leg movements seemed to be a struggle for him. Even just sucking on a bottle seemed to exhaust him. I truly had no idea what could be wrong. I thought he was just a little delayed, although I carried a heavy feeling deep inside my gut. I guess this is considered mother's intuition.

At the age of 4 months (just two weeks after the unforgettable 9/11) I took him to a pediatrician at Bethesda Naval Hospital, the United State Navy's primary medical treatment facility. This was the closest hospital to the base that the Army referred to for specialists. The news that day would change the course of my life forever. As the pediatrician examined him I could see the worry on her face. She left the room and returned in what felt like hours to tell me that she was fairly certain Steven had a disease called Spinal Muscular Atrophy (SMA). She wanted to have the pediatrician that was on rounds that day in the clinic confirm the diagnosis. I had no idea what that meant, but it didn't sound good. I thought "I can handle a handicapped child just as long as he is with me." The pediatrician proceeded to tell me that he had the worst form, Type I or Werdnig Hoffman Disease, of this little known genetic disease and that he would most likely not live to celebrate his first birthday. You see, there was NO treatment or cure.

"Spinal muscular atrophy (SMA) is a disease that robs people of physical strength by affecting the motor nerve cells in the spinal cord, taking away the ability to walk, eat, or breathe. It is the number one genetic cause of death for infants.

SMA is caused by a mutation in the survival motor neuron gene 1 (SMN1). In a healthy person, this gene produces a protein that is critical to the function of the nerves that control our muscles. Without it, those nerve cells cannot properly function and eventually die, leading to debilitating and sometimes fatal muscle weakness. SMA affects approximately 1 in 11,000 births, and about 1 in every 50 Americans is a genetic carrier. SMA can affect any race or gender.

There are four primary types of SMA—1, 2, 3, and 4—based on the age that symptoms begin, and the highest physical milestone achieved.

Individuals with SMA have difficulty performing the basic functions of life, like breathing and swallowing. However, SMA does not affect a person's ability to think, learn, and build relationships with others.
(source:https://www.curesma.org/about-sma/)

The Pediatric Neurologist that confirmed the diagnosis coldly told me to take him home and love him the best I could because his days were limited. Those words still play in my head today. I vividly recall the car ride home as my mom tried to hold back her tears. On that perfect crisp Fall-like day, I sat in the back sobbing as I held Steven's little finger gazing into his beautiful blue eyes and thought how can this be real?

As you can imagine breaking the news to my husband Jason was horrible. I recall him feeling disbelief and shock because just hours before our baby boy was "perfectly" healthy. As he stood in his Army battle dress uniform, the strong and unbreakable man that I always knew broke down. Despite Steven's diagnosis, Jay was my rock throughout the coming months and years. He would be there by my side doing the things I couldn't bring myself to do. For example, when Steven had to be admitted to the hospital to get his feeding tube placed, I literally couldn't stay with him as I was terrified he would die through the procedure. Jay didn't leave Steven's side and picked up when and where I was not strong enough to. God knew we needed each other to get through the hardest storm in our young married lives.

As I stood in the shower that evening I felt no need to ever get out. Maybe if I stay in here long enough, this will all be a bad dream. All of my wishes and dreams for my future, Steven's future, my family's future vanished into thin air. But no, this is my new reality. As I exit the shower the fog is still there. For my children's sake, I had to get myself together and put on my mask of bravery, whatever that was supposed to look like. In reality what I had was a swollen red face and bulging eyes from endless tears.

Running and showers became my only escape from dealing with the heaviness of my living nightmare. Running had been therapy for me since the age of 14, so I felt this was a safe way to channel the pain in a private way.

For the next six months all my showers were the same. I spent as much time as I could letting the water drench me until my body was pruned. These were literally the only minutes during the day I could have to myself and think. The water from the showerhead concealed my tears. In fact, some days I think more tears flowed from my eyes, than water from the shower.

Steven's Days

Watching Steven struggle to breathe each day was almost unbearable. It was torture. I had to perform medical tasks that I never imagined doing. My days were spent suctioning the mucous that he couldn't clear, feeding him through his gastrointestinal tube, and constantly palpating his delicate chest to help him breathe. Therapists came in and out of the house, moving his delicate limbs. My heart felt as if it had been ripped from my chest. I shouldn't have to perform these things on anyone but especially my own child. Fortunately, we brought hospice in to help keep Steven as comfortable as possible. The nurse (I can still remember her name -Tommi) truly was a gift from God and had such a compassionate heart. In addition, we were so blessed that Steven's pediatrician, Dr. Olnes, made house calls when we felt scared and desperate.

I felt gratitude for the smallest things like rocking him in my arms, reading books to him, singing to him. I reflect on the bible verse Psalm 147:7:

> *Sing to the Lord with grateful praise;*
> *make music to our God on the harp.*

No matter the pain I was experiencing singing brought joy in the littlest moments. My favorite song to sing to him was *You are My Sunshine*. I held his little hands and looked into his big blue angel eyes, just mesmerized by my angel on Earth.

We were generally quarantined to the house from the day he was diagnosed until the day he passed, other than short visits outside so he could experience a snowfall or see the sunset. One trip we did take was to our local mall. I vividly remember carrying Steven onto the beautiful carousel and thinking this will be the only time he will experience an amusement ride in his life. He was mesmerized by the shimmering colors and lights. I could see his wonder in his eyes.

We celebrated everything we could, including each month's birthday, his only ride on the tractor to pick a pumpkin, and Christmas. Even though we knew he wouldn't be with us long, we bought him lots of presents for Christmas morning and made it as festive as possible. Every experience we had in those short months would be his first and last. Isobel was only two at the time, so keeping her occupied and having her spend as much time with Steven was so important. This was a struggle all on its own, but it was as if Isobel knew and granted us simplicity in taking care of her. She was very content just "being."

I was extremely blessed by our family and a few close friends who did not shy away from the fear of seeing Steven, knowing full well that it could be their last visit with him. Our families rotated days visiting Steven as they wanted to spend as much time with him as possible.

My youngest sister Justine selflessly moved from Portland, Oregon to live with us for a couple of months. She was a huge support for me particularly with Isobel so I could focus more on Steven's round the clock care. When I asked her why she chose to do this for me, she said, "I felt like I had a purpose. Like my life left me free at that very moment in time so I could be there. I felt blessed that I could help you. You were always there for me and I was happy to be there for you. It gave me a special time with Isobel which I will never forget. I am so grateful that I was able to know Steven in a more intimate setting than if I was just visiting. In my mind it was obvious that it was where I was meant to be."

My in-laws would drive eight hours round trip, from Northeastern Pennsylvania, in a day just to hold him and offer support to us. My father-in-law would take time off from work as a Superintendent and stay for days at a time helping us with Steven and Isobel. He had a very special bond with his grandson, after all Steven was named after "Poppy Moyer." In fact, the early morning that Steven passed, Poppy and Grandma Moyer were with us as well.

Steven coded several times throughout his last few months. I truly can't describe what that was like but I believe in my heart he knew when his time to leave would be "right." We had to order a DNR or a do not resuscitate order because we chose palliative care for our boy. We couldn't stand to see him suffer longer than when God called him home.

On Valentine's Day 2002, I held Steven's tiny little hand, looked into his baby blue eyes and told him it was ok to let go. I sang to him and played music. Isobel held balloons for him to marvel at and we just embraced the moments as I knew in my heart he was near the end of his Earthly journey.

Two weeks later, just as my older brother Ron's daughter Lily was entering the world in the late hours of March 1st, Steven was leaving it. Early on that cold rainy morning of

March 2nd of 2002 our son died. It's as if he knew it was the day of Lily's birth so he fought just a little longer so he would not pass on the same day. This was a concern for me when I knew my niece's due date and I prayed that God would listen to my request for the death and birth not to be on the same day. His little body couldn't fight anymore and he was at peace. This was just the beginning of a long painful journey to healing. Steven's battle was over and my internal war would rage for a long time.

Just hours later my parents arrived to be with us and I vividly remember my Dad just cradling me in his arms as tears flowed silently from his face. It breaks my heart to this day to think our parents had to watch us mourn the loss of their grandson and watch their own children go through hell. That is what it felt like if I imagine what Hell is like. The minutes, hours, and days immediately following Steven's death (I hate this word because it is so final) were tormenting and torturous to say the least. The overwhelming emptiness and grief felt like I was drowning with no life vest to save me. No parent should ever have to bury their child!

I share this eulogy because I am so proud of the legacy Steven left despite his short time on Earth.

These were my Dad's words at Steven's funeral:

"Families and their friends gather together for christenings, Communions, Birthdays, Holidays, weddings and at these sad moments.

Eulogies are meant for those whose lives here had longevity-years of accomplishments-

No matter how simple they may have been.

This Eulogy is for too brief a life.
That life of Steven.
Gone from us too soon.
But packed into his days, one short of nine months, was more life, strength,
Courage and love
That many lives never experience in 90-plus years.
In these times when life itself means so little to many
Life in All its stages from the early
Conceived and unborn to the elderly
Steven's life has meant so much.
His life for the most part was in the gleam of his dancing eyes-
That we all cherished
Eyes that told us so much.
Strength & Courage were bound as one with Steven.
As his body weakened- he always fought-
Three times fighting back from the brink-
In order to give a few more days of joy
To those who loved and cared for him.
And his strength encourage were matched only by that of Jessica and Jason - Whose deeds we could only hope to do
During those long months.

With Steven, love on a human level
Reached a new high.
Although he could never talk to say the words we would want to hear
Nor could he return a hug to show he cared
He gave back all the love he got
With his gaze, with his eyes, his
Weakened smile.
And almost like a wise old man

He knew it all-
He knew everything we wanted him to know-
That he was loved
And so he shall be-
always."

One of the many lessons I learned from Steven's life on Earth is love knows no boundaries. It will carry on through time and space. It is intangible however present at all times. I think of the Winnie the Pooh quote, "You may be gone from my sight, but you are never gone from my heart." I carry Steven with me every minute of every hour of every day until my days on this planet are over. Then we will be reunited.

Chapter 2

*"The worst wound a person can experience
is the loss of a piece of their being-heart and soul"
-Jessica Moyer*

And just like that... I was in the club I never imagined I would be part of. I didn't realize this group of people (parents who have lost a child) could become part of my life. This club never seeks members, however when you join this group you so desperately need them. How could this happen to me? What did I do to deserve this indescribable pain and how was I ever going to heal? I was left with so many questions and few answers. After all there is no book, no list, no laid out plan on what to do when you lose part of your being. It is not the normal course of life to bury your child. I had no idea how I would carry on with life after watching a piece of me leave. The absence of his presence was almost too much bear.

Eventually, I would discover that the short beautiful life of my sweet son was truly a blessing from above. I soon learned that this unwanted club was a part of way too many parents and their lives. However, despite the sadness I would experience for years to come, I would also discover the purpose of my pain that I just needed to slowly unwrap over time. Let's face it, time and resilience are the tools we have to slowly heal the wounds and replace our sorrow with joy.

Life goes on whether you want it to or not and whether you participate or not.

Autopilot set in. I had another child who needed me more than ever. In reality, I needed her more than she will ever know. She was a busy two year old who didn't want to sit still and had no idea what was going on. How do you explain to your toddler that her baby brother is not coming back? She would ask where did Steven go? She wanted to play with his little toys and hold his little hand. My explanation was the best I could give at the time. Steven went to heaven because God needed some special angels.

He will always be with you although you can't see him.

How do you teach faith to a young child? In the coming months and years Jay and I talked openly about her brother Steven and our conviction that he was now an angel in Heaven. We truly believed in our hearts that he was at peace and no longer suffering. When I talk to Isobel now (she is 21) about her memories and how she feels like her brother's death shaped our family this is what she stated:

I don't have any memory or detailed recollection of Steven being alive. Maybe I do deep in my memory but no matter how hard I think about it, I can only recall what the VHS tapes and photos portrayed of us. Steven was so close in age to me, two years to be exact, however I never got the chance to really know him. A horrific disease took him away from my family at such a young age, which would later become a transformational event in shaping who my family is today.

Throughout my life my brother Steven has been a symbol of strength for me. It pains me that he endured suffering throughout his time on earth, but I often remind myself of his bright blue eyes and beautiful smile. His smile was contagious, even at such a young age he could light up a room. In the low points of my life, he has been my inspiration and protector when I find myself losing hope or motivation.

I have always wished that he could have grown up by my side and been able to live a full life. Often asking myself, what could have been. The unknown of who he could have been in life is something I struggle with constantly. However, throughout life I have always felt his spirit with me. Despite the short time I spent with him, I have always felt connected and that he is always with me. His passing was not only transformational in how I live, but affected my parents' lives forever.

My mom has continued to keep Steven's spirit alive by commemorating his life with organizing events, fundraisers and reshaping her life's purpose. Growing up, my mom has distinctly always made a point to emphasize that she has four kids, despite the loss of Steven. The grief and sadness that consumed my mom eventually became a building block for her to empower the lives of other people. The love and admiration I have towards my mom is immeasurable. She continues to inspire myself and others, acting as a friend and beacon of light to whoever is blessed with her presence. She is a great example of selflessness and perseverance even when she has received the worst of life- losing a child.

I know that she will always carry the weight of Steven's loss with her but also all of the lessons and love that it has taught her. My mom is a warrior and survivor all in one. I could not be more proud of the person that my mom has become and continue to push personal and professional boundaries throughout life. I will forever miss my brother Steven and always wish that he was with me, however I know he is my angel watching over our family. I am eternally thankful that I have the ability to call him my brother and my love for him is unparalleled. Steven's short nine months on earth has taught everyone many lessons and has shaped my family into who they are today. My beautiful brother continues to impact all who have and will hear his story.

Just two weeks after Steven passed we took Isobel on an Easter train ride. It was the oddest feeling to do something "normal" when nothing in life felt normal. I felt extreme guilt for just not wallowing in my tears 24/7. As I watched other parents joyfully engaging with their kids, I felt such torment. Anywhere I went I felt like wearing a note on me saying "I just lost my child so please do not approach." Carrying on with normalcy was a daily struggle. Some days just getting dressed or going to the store required enormous effort. This is where you just blindly put one foot in front of the other and go into robot mode. The minutes turn to hours, then days, then weeks and before you know it months have gone by. All the while, time seems to stand still.

A couple months went by and my husband and I were encouraged to seek grief counseling. Many people cautioned us that the divorce rate was quite high for those couples who lost a child. I think most people will agree that men and women do not grieve the same way and this became a challenge for us. We were clearly handling our loss differently. He would keep everything bottled up and I would just be mean and angry.

I felt resentment because he had a real job and got to escape the day-to-day realities. I had to fill the void and entertain our daughter, pretending I was happy. Because we were a military family with the military's medical insurance, our choices in therapy were limited.

Sitting in the counselor's office I tried to have an open mind, but let's face it, how is someone who has never lived through such trauma supposed to give advice to those of us that have? After two visits I was done. Please don't think I am saying counseling and therapy is a bad idea. I know it can be therapeutic and necessary for many to work through various life issues and traumas. However, at this time in my life I didn't feel this would move me forward or help me work through my grief. I found no value in it and sought solace from other moms who understood my loss. This undesirable "club" was now my therapy and one of the best ways to recognize that my feelings were valid. I am forever indebted to those who supported us and understood the depths of our pain.

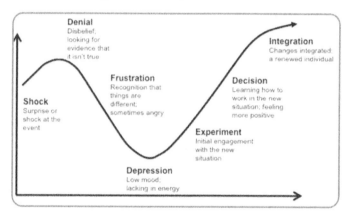

As I was recently speaking with others who have experienced grief and loss, one friend mentioned the Kubler-Ross Grief Cycle. This cycle refers to the five stages of grief including denial, anger, bargaining, depression and acceptance. This theory was developed by Elisabeth Kubler-Ross in 1969 who was a Swiss Psychiatrist. Surprisingly I was not too familiar with what this graph was and honestly many years ago didn't know there were charts for the "stages of grief." I never had a reason to seek out what I would experience or how I should feel. I just went through the motions and emotions.

After looking at this chart, I guess this is what it truly was like to experience anguish and live through it. I recognized that I started the stages of grief as soon as Steven was diagnosed, honestly maybe even a little before because deep in my soul I knew something was terribly wrong.

I don't necessarily believe that the order is exact and you may waver back and forth between the stages for a long time. That's why this cycle resembles a wave. The ups and downs of grief will present over the rest of your life in the most unlikely of times. I guess it makes you feel normal when you know that these are the emotions and feelings that most feel when they experience agony. I think the hardest part of grief, may be surrendering to the pain and embracing the "hurt" as that exemplifies what love truly is.

I must note: Although I experienced most or all of these feelings in no particular order, not everyone experiencing loss will. Just like anything in life, we all react differently to our pain and therefore there is no right or wrong way to fluctuate through grief.

I believe that a sense of mourning carries on the rest of our lives, and the tears will flow at the most unexpected times. I have trust what the Scriptures say, *'He will wipe*

every tear from their eyes. There will be no more death'
or mourning or crying or pain, for the old order of things
has passed away." He who was seated on the throne said,
"I am making everything new!" Then he said, "Write this
down, for these words are trustworthy and true."
- Revelation 21:4-5

At some point you will notice the tears will lessen and that
love and hope will flourish!

I Couldn't Sit Still
(The purpose starts to unfold)

Because of Steven's presence in my life, I decided to take
action in some way. I couldn't stand by and do nothing. I had
to pour my sadness and energy into something worthwhile!

I was fortunate to know other moms "in the club" who
supported me through these difficult times. After Steven
was diagnosed with SMA, I immediately felt a need to
connect with other parents who had experienced what I
was about to go through. Although every child's experience
with this disease is different I sought out any resource I
could find to help me. Barbara and Julie, were local SMA
"angel moms" and were extremely supportive to our family.
They both were very active in fundraising, outreach and
education. With their inspiration and my family's support,
in February of 2002, I decided to start a local chapter of
Cure Spinal Muscular Atrophy.

I poured my grief into fundraising. Our first event in the
summer of 2002, Steven's Gala for a Cure, brought in close
to $40,000 and I felt incredibly blessed by the amount
of support. Let's face it, most people have no clue how to

respond to a parent who has lost a child, so for many this was their way of showing their empathy. Because Steven's passing was so recent, hundreds of family and friends showed up willing to donate and rally behind our cause.

Because I was now a chapter leader, my information was public and part of my journey of healing was to support others. I just didn't realize it would be so soon. Only a couple weeks after Steven passed I received a call from a mom in Florida who had just been told her baby boy had SMA. As I listened to this mom, my heart was breaking for her knowing what was to come for her beautiful baby boy. I could only offer a shoulder to cry on and the best practices to keep Steven comfortable. I broke down after that call, but deep down I knew that God was beckoning me to be his servant.

Through the years, my husband and I have counseled and supported many families. Despite those feelings that build up in my heart, I know 100% that this is part of my journey to growth and healing.

Talking with other parents somewhat hardened me though. I became so good at separating my emotions and compartmentalizing my feelings. Having these heart-wrenching conversations and knowing the outcome for these children affected by such a terrible disease was necessary but mentally and physically exhausting. It was difficult at that time to offer hope when there was no cure or treatment, yet.

Comforting Others Through My Grief

You know when something tragic happens in your life and you think the whole world stops? I am here to tell you it doesn't. Life carries on despite your world crumbling. I had to tolerate the most inconsiderate comments from some people such as, "Well you can have more children" as if another one would be a replacement like a light bulb. Or "Do you know what the divorce rate is for a couple who loses a child?" According to research through Compassionate Friends, surprisingly it is only about 16-18%. Everyone else went on with their life even though mine felt like it ended. Frankly, it felt like more of a blow because I had already lost so much!

Saying most people don't know how to react to someone who has lost a child is truly an understatement. It's as if the passing of a child is contagious. After Steven's death, I felt like all of a sudden people were avoiding me. Some of the friends I once had slowly started to disappear into the shadows. Many times I avoided social events because I felt like people were watching my every movement or avoiding me because they had no idea what to say.

As a "fixer" I almost felt a responsibility to make people feel okay with my loss so they wouldn't get emotional. I didn't cry in front of people and remained quite stoic because this is how I would protect myself from a public display of a possible breakdown.

What I didn't realize until I was in this club, I was not alone and too many parents had experienced the loss of their child. You know when you buy a car and then all of a sudden you see the same one everywhere? As I shared that I had a son who passed, many parents who had lost a child started opening up. My transparency gave others the permission to tell their story of loss, whether it was a miscarriage, the death of a child or a relative or close friend. What irony!

I found myself comforting or protecting others from my pain because it was easier that way. As a "fixer" I almost felt a responsibility to make people feel okay with my loss so they wouldn't get emotional.

So many moms I have spoken to through the years have suffered miscarriages. This loss is detrimental for these women and men too. As soon as we know we are pregnant the hopes and dreams for our unborn child begin! What most people (even some closest to me) don't know is that I was pregnant towards the end of Steven's battle. Just a couple days before he passed, I testified at The National Institute of Health about my son's battle with this devastating genetic disease and how funds were desperately needed to find a cure. I remember thinking my body did not feel right that day. The day after Steven's funeral as I was laying at my in-laws house, I started to miscarry. Honestly I have blocked so much of those days "after" but clearly my body was in such a state of stress it just wasn't capable of carrying another child. I had been through the worst so not much could shake me at that time. I was so devastated over just burying my child that I didn't feel much else at the time. It was literally one foot in front of another for so many days!

The word surreal comes to mind as I think back to this life that seems so long ago, yet still like yesterday. Was it really me who experienced such trauma at such a young age and how did I not just survive but thrive and find joy and happiness again? My ideas, suggestions and tools to come later on.

Surreal

My life continued to be surreal. Here I go again. That summer

I became pregnant yet again (getting pregnant was never the issue). At 12 weeks I had Chorionic Villus Sampling (CVS), which is the removal of a piece of placenta for genetic testing to see if this baby would be affected by SMA.

There was a 1 in 4 chance that the baby could be affected, it was a roll of the dice each time I got pregnant. Of course I was terrified but never in my wildest dreams thought my luck could be this bad. The baby tested positive for SMA and after tough conversations with my husband we decided to terminate within a few days. I know many people are judging me right now and that's understandable. It was hard enough to deal with my own guilt let alone other people's reactions or opinions. Laying in the cold, sterile, white hospital room listening to the nurses whisper, was a somber experience I will never forget. Not one of them knew my story, not one of them knew the suffering my son had to bear, not one of them understood the pain as a mom to watch the slow unbearable death of her own son. I had to let the judgement go. I knew deep in my heart I was not capable of surviving if I had to watch another child die.

As if losing Steven and having a miscarriage the day after his funeral wasn't enough, I had to work through the anger and confusion of this. I stepped into my "confessional" that evening and had an angry conversation with God. How could he put me in this situation and how could I learn to forgive myself? I was taught as a lifelong Catholic that the "A" word (abortion) was a grave sin. I just cried in disbelief. The emotions poured out of me right into the drain and as I towel-dried I put on my "tough" skin. Maybe this would be the night I had to give myself grace and forgiveness. To this day, I struggle with the decisions I felt forced to make, however I trust in God's pardon and mercy.

Later that year, in the summer of 2002, we moved to Fort Drum, New York. My husband was in the Army and we were given the choice to have a change in assignment.. I was so happy to have a change of scenery, but despite the move my sadness didn't lessen. I thought moving to a different place would help ease some of the familiar pain but instead it isolated me a bit more.

Here I was in a new place. No one knew my story and I got to choose who I had the energy to tell and more so who I felt "deserved" to hear it. It was exhausting to deal with comforting others and making them feel okay when I told them I had a son pass away. Many times I chose not to reveal that deep loss so I could avoid the uncomfortable silence or awkwardness.

I was fortunate that my daughter gave me a purpose. After all, she relied on me for everything. At the time of Steven's passing she was not quite three. I had to make a decision; even though I felt like I wanted to die along with my son some days, I had many reasons to live. My sweet little Isobel gave me that reason and kept my mind distracted from the dark clouds that never seemed to vanish. I created so many memories with her. She was my sidekick and I poured my energy into her every need. We made the best of our new house in upstate New York. I have such fond memories of playing Lion King, Care Bears, and Mickey Mouse House with her. I clung on to the few constants in my life. I always had an uneasy, anxious feeling that something would happen to take more loved ones away from me.

Chapter 3

As If Things Couldn't Get Worse...

*"Courage is not having the strength
to go on, it's going on when you
don't have the strength."*
-Theodore Roosevelt

It is written in the Bible that God only gives you what you can handle and I've always learned to trust God. But really, c'mon. Somehow, this was feeling to me like a cruel joke.

My husband Jay is a good man. I truly am incredibly blessed. We met in Erie, Pennsylvania the winter of January 1996. He swept me off my feet during a snowball fight at college and we got engaged just ten months after dating. I always told him he was my knight in shining armor. I just knew we were meant to be together and I still feel this way twenty three years later. We married December 20, 1997 at St. Mary Magdalen de Pazzi, the first national Italian Parish in the United States founded in 1852 in Philadelphia. The priest, Father Natali, actually  married my parents as well and was a close family friend. Surrounded by a few hundred people, we took our vows including through good times and in bad never imaging how "bad" life could truly be. We had the most beautiful wedding reception at The Ballroom at the Ben. I felt as if God knew we were going to endure so much together so he gave us each other. We lost our child and he was the only person who knew that pain. The three of us (Isobel, Jay, and I) were inseparable after Steven passed. We clung so deeply to each other.

My husband's duty station, the 10th Mountain Division, was one of the most highly deployable units in the U.S. Army. Although I knew there was a high probability he would get deployed I think I was in denial. Luck never seemed to be on my side, at least that was my mindset. Sure enough, Jay got the call that he would be deploying to Afghanistan the summer we were due with our third child. Fortunately, this baby tested negative when I had the CVS test and although an emotional and sick pregnancy, I was nervously excited expecting another baby. Here I was 7 months pregnant in the middle of nowhere, so far away from family with very little to do with limited support raising a four year old.

The night before his deployment, we headed to my parents in New Jersey. Isobel and I and the soon-to-be new baby were going to stay with them while Jay was gone. I didn't want to leave my surroundings and face yet another tumultuous uncertain time. So I submerged myself in my tiny bath. I sat in the tub for hours filling it up with my own water that poured from my eyes. I felt so overwhelmed and angry that I was going to give birth to our second son and he would be on the other side of the world in a warzone. The panic, anger and fear were crippling. He literally had to pull me from the tub because I knew that once I got out the beginning of a new painful journey was beginning. I should have been over the moon that I would be welcoming another child into the world but instead I felt like the ground had been pulled out from under me yet again. I think of the quote by Theodore Roosevelt, "Courage is not having the strength to go on; it's going on when you don't have the strength." I was truly terrified that I was not strong enough to go through the next six months to a year alone. Despite how forlorn and weak I felt, I had to put my brave pants on at least for the sake of my children.

I love my parents and was so appreciative of their support but the added stress of not being in my own home with my husband was a lot to bear. The morning Blaise was born, Jay was on the phone as I was giving birth with both of my parents by my side. He should have been with me. Instead he was sitting in New York waiting to board an aircraft for Afghanistan at any moment. I clearly remember checking myself out of the hospital less than 24 hours after Blaise's birth because I was beside myself with absolute anguish. I wanted to be with Isobel as she was my only constant at the time.

After Blaise's birth I sunk into a deeper depression. I was probably suffering from postpartum depression while also comparing every little breath of his to Steven's, worrying that something was wrong with him too. I reached my breaking point four months into my husband's deployment. I am embarrassed to admit that I felt suicidal. I couldn't eat, or couldn't sleep. I vividly recall talking myself out of sitting in the garage with my car running to just put me to sleep and out of my misery. The only escape I had again was in the shower or on a run. It was in those moments I concluded I had to seek out medical help. I believe my parents knew I was sad, but I don't think at that time they understood the overwhelming desperation I was experiencing. The doctor recognized how bad my mental and physical state was and soon after evaluations, my husband was notified to return. This was truly humbling. I prided myself on being such a strong resilient woman and the act of having him return because I was a wreck felt very shameful. I encourage my readers to seek help immediately if you ever experience distressed suicidal thoughts!

This is where the word Grace stepped in. I did not ask for all of these horrible life experiences. I had to acknowledge that I was weakened by my son's death, my other two pregnancy losses and the deployment. I felt judged by the military wives but to be honest, they did not walk in my shoes and they did not know my story. I had to get over what others thought of me and accept that I needed some normalcy in my life in order to heal.

Life continued to teach me lessons. I learned I was not in control of much and that just like me, so many others are suffering a battle that we may know nothing about. It is so important to give others grace and just offer a hand to hold, an ear to listen and a hug to embrace.

Jay returned shortly after Thanksgiving. We moved back to Fort Drum to finish his military obligation and together made the decision that he would leave the military life behind after his commitment was up. We needed to rebuild our lives.

In the summer of 2004, we moved to Delaware and started a new chapter in our life. Little did I know that my heart was about to be tested a few more times.

When I stepped in the shower in my new home in Delaware I could spend time away from the world just lost in my own thoughts. I felt a sense of comfort knowing that I would finally feel settled for a long period of time. Not knowing a soul (again), I could have a fresh start.

I was fortunate to stay home with my children while they were younger. After Jay got out of the military we moved to this little state where he started a "normal" career in an ophthalmology practice. Although closer to our families again, I was starting over. Shortly after we moved I got pregnant with my son Jake. I had to wait 13 weeks to make sure he was not affected with SMA. Once I got the news he was healthy I was overjoyed! For once I felt like I may have a little normalcy! I settled into a homemaker and mom routine and joined the local YMCA. I found comfort in exercise and self-care.

I didn't always practice self-care. For many of my younger years I sabotaged my body. At 13 years old, my showers became a place where I would shame my body, a safe place where I could hide my bony frame from everyone. I would suck in my stomach and make sure I could still palpate my ribs. If I could feel the bones protruding I knew I hadn't gained weight. As a competitive gymnast for several years I became obsessed with my body fat and measurements. Every day we walked into the gym I would have to step on the scale and get my skin pinched. Of course as an impressionable teenager obsessed with pleasing everyone I made sure I didn't gain weight. Fortunately my parents recognized the rapid decline of my health and sought help for me. I had to give up the only sport and hobby I knew and loved. For over six years my life revolved around gymnastics. My identity was a gymnast. I sought refuge in the shower where my tears could flow freely and I could hide the hollow pain from my family. The sadness and shame I felt was eventually replaced by focusing on getting healthy again since I found a new sport in high school - cross country.

When I felt overwhelmed, next to showers, running was my jam! After Steven passed away I decided I would run a marathon in his memory to raise awareness for the disease that stole him from me. I found a purpose through my pain. I trained for five months and completed my first marathon -The Marine Corps marathon in Washington, DC. I find it quite appropriate that this popular 26.2 mile race's motto is "Run with Purpose, finish with Pride!" Of course in my mind I thought how hard can it really be?

Well darn, I hit the runners wall (depletion of glycogen store, depletion of energy and serious fatigue) at 18 miles. I will never forget a woman coming up behind me as I was barely moving. She put her hand on my back, where I had a picture of my baby, and she said "Do it for Steven!"

If I could have found her in the crowd of 20,000 people after the race I would have hugged her. I was so grateful for just those 4 words - Do it for Steven. Those words, along with grit, carried me through the remaining miles. That night as I flopped my weary worn-out body into the shower, I wept tears of satisfaction and gratitude. I felt so accomplished and knew my baby would be so proud. I am pleased to say that to this date I have run eight marathons and a few triathlons in Steven's memory.

Running was one of my good habits to deal with the emotional pain. When we suffer from loss, we can find ourselves going down some dark paths and creating habits that may not necessarily serve us. I have watched many grieving people turn to alcohol, drugs, food, gambling or self-deprecation just to name a few. For me I used exercise to help ward off the anguish which was great and helpful during the day, but at night when alone with my thoughts trying to sleep, my mind wouldn't stop. It's as if there was a constant tick of a clock and I couldn't shut it off. I turned first to over the counter sleep remedies and when they stopped working I moved on to prescription medications. I just didn't want to think anymore. It was a vicious cycle. I am going to be transparent here - occasionally I still need these medications to help me sleep, but again I need to allow myself grace that I have suffered through major traumas and I am not perfect.

However, I am proud of myself for acknowledging my shortcomings and working to find a solution by replacing these bad habits with better, healthier ones.

Chapter 4

The Hits Kept Coming

"What we have once enjoyed we can never lose.
All that we love deeply becomes part of us."
-Helen Keller

I step in the only space I feel safe to protect my children from the sobs that are about to explode out of me. I am preparing myself to say goodbye to my hero, my confidante, my Dad. He will forever be part of my essence because he gifted me so many of the qualities I bestow.

Today I will drive to New Jersey to watch him be removed from life support and watch him take his final breath on this Earth. How appropriate that it is *Good Friday* 2008. Dad was a man of faith and conviction and how ironic he would pass the same day as Jesus. I think God must be telling us something, right? I snap myself back to reality and as the water turns cold, so does my blood. It is as if I am being prepared for the torture ahead. I knew as soon as I got out, I would have to face reality and make the sobering drive to the hospital.

When Steven was diagnosed our parents were our rocks. They would drop everything to be with us if we needed them. I had a very special relationship with my Dad. Although we did not see eye to eye on everything, he instilled in me a sense of purpose early on in my life. As a primary care doctor I watched him care for thousands of patients with such a loving, generous heart. He was the doctor you would see on tv shows; one of the few who would make house calls in the middle of the night or sit with families after they lost a loved one and comfort them. Dad was the foundation of our family.

The one everyone wanted to be around. He was the life of the party. He made everyone feel welcome. As a cross country runner in high school and college, I knew that my Dad would be somewhere on the trail. Despite how busy he was he made sure to take time to cheer me on! When I heard him exclaim "Let's Go Jessie Meg!", my pace would automatically shift into overdrive.

My dad was the calm to the storm. He was a man of beautiful wisdom and words. He wrote this poem after Steven passed:

Steven

He took his leave not long ago
It seems such a little while
He left me with my head in my hand
Thinking of his Smile

A smile that said I love you
Only if my little lips could kiss you
Indeed I took my leave
Just know, please know
How much I miss you.

Come back to me again tonight
On summer winds through my window
Whisper some soothing words to me
Before the winter winds blow.

And when I wake some morning
May my heart be filled with hope and joy
Knowing that I will always love you
Forever mine, my little Boy.

Unfortunately my Dad took care of everyone but himself. He worked sixty plus hours a week to provide for our family, was a smoker for many years,did not exercise regularly and his diet was not ideal. Just a few years after Steven passed my father was diagnosed with pulmonary fibrosis, a lung disease with no treatment or cure. Once again facing the reality of finality. He was the type of man that would not complain or allow others to help. I pleaded with him so many times to just take better care of himself! He battled through lung cancer and a quadruple bypass but his body eventually started to give out. I still feel the sting of tears today as I write, thirteen years later.

As hard as losing my father was, I had faith that he was with Steven. Now, I was left to not only pick up what was left of my heart, but to support my mom who just lost her best friend of over fifty years. Again there is no right or wrong way to go through the journey of grief. Over the years I have witnessed so many different paths to healing. During this time I felt I needed to put my own feelings aside and dig in to support my mom. Time felt like it stood still. I went through the motions of life but I wasn't really feeling like I was living again. My Dad was the glue of the family and since he was gone I felt like life started to unravel again. I felt when my Dad passed, a big part of my mom was suddenly gone too. Here I was, trying to be strong for my mom, but inside I could barely keep it together. Once again, I felt like I was in robot mode. I didn't feel present while taking care of three children, and this still bothers me. I kept up the household, trying to keep my mom occupied, and yet felt like I was failing miserably in all aspects. I found the best way to deal with grief was to pour myself into something that would challenge and grow me the following year.

Through my love and passion for fitness and health, I became certified as a group fitness instructor a year after my Dad passed. Oddly enough, my mom mentioned going to a Zumba Fitness certification training since we both loved dance. My mom, sisters, and I spent many years in dance classes and entertaining in retirement homes with our awesome dance moves. Little did I know this day would help carve out my future path. Dance was a way to work through the sadness and pain and help others get into better shape. I found music and movement as therapy for me and many others!

Steven had no control over his health, so I became almost obsessed with preaching self-care to others. Most people get to choose how they will take care of their health, and it became my message. I started to develop my purpose, and through exercise, I was able to be generous with my talents. I found great satisfaction and personal growth from leading a variety of fitness classes at many local gyms. I started to emerge from my cocoon and relax a bit. I became more involved in giving back to the local community in many ways. Life really began to feel normal, and I started to feel joy again!

Chapter 5

*"Be on your guard, stand firm in the
faith; be courageous; be strong"*
-1 Corinthians 16:13

As I was teaching a fitness class at the local YMCA, I noticed my phone kept buzzing and when I finished the class I saw several missed calls. I immediately called my sister back and she was screaming into the phone. My heart sank. My mom suffered a stroke and was airlifted to a trauma hospital. How could this be possible? She seemed completely healthy and happy just a few days ago at a fundraiser she hosted in memory of Steven.

My mom was the spearhead behind me starting the local chapter of Cure SMA. Mom is the creative genius in the family, always coming up with new fun ideas for her five kids and eleven grandchildren. She never seems to age to me because she is non-stop full of energy. So when Steven was diagnosed we needed to find a way to pour the tremendous pain we were feeling into something positive. For the past 18 years she has poured her heart and soul into fundraising through various events throughout the local communities.

I immediately ran home, grabbed my family and we rushed to New Jersey. When I got to the hospital I knew by the look on everyone's faces that this was a life-threatening situation. We were told that she might not live. Pause. How in the world was this possible? I was in shock! I had lost my son, my dad and now my mom may not live. Life just didn't seem fair again! As the family gathered together we held onto one another and just prayed for God to intercede and save the women who raised five healthy children, cared for everyone, loved my Dad beyond words and adored her grandkids. In what felt like hours, the doctor returned and explained she had suffered a massive stroke in the frontal lobe of her brain. They didn't know what to expect but she was stable.

Honestly I blocked so much out that the details are sketchy. As we went to see her in the Intensive Care Unit, she was almost unrecognizable. Although conscious she was not there. She babbled words we couldn't decipher and she was in horrific pain. After a week she was stable enough to be discharged. My mom is a stubborn woman and refused to go to a nursing facility so with much hesitation we brought her back to her house. For a few weeks we tended to her every need. My youngest sister was with her day and night because she was terrified of losing her. Just when we thought she may start improving she suffered seizures. She was again rushed to the ICU. When my sister called, I was once again brought to my knees.

As I crawled into my prayer box, - the shower, I pleaded with God to heal her. I couldn't face the loss of my mom! I held so many conversations with God here. This day I was bartering with him. I am not sure what I was offering him in return but this is all I could do at the time.

My siblings and I were shocked when they told us she now suffered a blood clot in the back part of her brain. Again, we were faced with the thought that she may not make it and if she did what quality of life would she have. Myself and my siblings grew up in a Catholic family so we believed in the power of prayers. She was in so many prayer chains and lifted up by so many. By the sheer grace of God, my mom was once again discharged. For several months following we took turns caring for her. We basically had to teach her everything, from identifying a fruit to writing a bill. My family did not give up on her. We found gratitude in the smallest wins-from my mom bathing herself to reading a few lines in the newspaper. Our family had grit and persevered through many enduring times! We kept on keeping on and today I am happy to report my mom is doing well and taking better care of herself.

As I tended to my mom throughout that year it brought me back to the time she helped me through horrible sickness when I was pregnant with my first born Isobel and also helped me care for Isobel during her first year. Shortly after I learned I was expecting, the vomiting began and I don't mean just a little morning sickness. I had severe hyperemesis. My sickness was so extreme that I was hospitalized and eventually had a picc line in my arm so when I got home from work as a pharmaceutical rep I would hook myself up and hydrate. I don't think I had one day during my pregnancy that I felt good. All I remember eating was pretzels and rice and sucked down lemonade. My mom was my constant during this time, tending to me and keeping me somewhat sane.

On July 3rd 1999, as I was sitting in my bed after I worked out, I felt a trickle down my leg. Hmm that's interesting, I thought, as I wasn't due for nine more weeks. Surely this was nothing to worry about. I called my parents

immediately and my Dad told me to head to the hospital-
that my water had broken. I still didn't understand the
gravity of the situation. I hopped in my watering hole with
my pregnant belly and bartered with God. Clearly, I had
many conversations in my prayer box.

God didn't answer my prayers like I hoped. Isobel was
born like a little firecracker on July 4th weighing in at a
whopping 3.4 lbs. Obviously I couldn't take her home
with me and walking out of the hospital without my little
girl was heart-wrenching. My womb was empty and so
were my arms. This was the first time in my life I think I
experienced overwhelming grief. I had to have trust in the
Neonatal intensive care unit (NICU) nurses that my baby
was in good hands. Getting in the shower when I returned
home, I looked down at my empty stomach and sobbed.
I felt I did something wrong to cause a premature birth
and I was angry. Over the next month I spent hours at
the hospital with my fragile girl hoping that every day she
would get stronger so I could bring her home where she
belonged. The day finally came and I was truly a nervous
wreck. Isobel had to be hooked up to monitors 24/7 for
the next six months. Every time it alarmed I would feel a
surge of anxiety worrying that she would stop breathing.
The anxiety became worse as I went back to work. I was so
blessed and grateful that I could leave her with my mom at
my father's practice, but I felt extreme guilt that I wasn't
with her all the time.

Let's talk about anxiety

Anxiety is the voice in your head that constantly alarms
you. When you go through stressful situations in life, things

keep repeating in your mind. It is like a song you hear that gets stuck on replay in your brain. Anxiety creates the "what ifs" that can drive you crazy.

Because of all the alarms attached to my little girl for the first six months and the health challenges Isobel could have faced in the first few years of her life, I became extremely anxious. As you can probably imagine after Steven passed my fears of sickness and death became almost unbearable. I was in a constant state of worry that the people I loved would get sick and die. For years after his death, I would check the kids several times a night to see if they were breathing. I would quietly sneak into their rooms and put my hand on their chest or ear near their mouth to confirm their breath. It was a vicious cycle that made me crazy! I was in serious mental distress.

I found myself running to the doctor whenever I experienced something out of the ordinary. I would take anything that felt wrong and automatically assume it was the worst case scenario. One particular example, the doctor ordered an x-ray of my shoulder because I was experiencing some numbing down my arm. When she called me with results she told me that they had identified a spot on my lung. Automatically I self diagnosed that I had pulmonary fibrosis or lung cancer like my Dad.

I got into the shower and cried myself silly thinking I was going to suffer and possibly die. Who would take care of my family? I had it all mapped out in my head. I sat for quite a long time and just wept. How many times do we get so wrapped up on what could happen instead of focusing on what we know to be true at that minute?

I needed to pull myself together. The next week went painfully slow as I waited for the results of the cat scan. Praise the Lord! It was a common finding on chest X-rays - a scar from a past pneumonia. I needed to stop the insanity of jumping to conclusions and thinking the worst case scenario for everything. But how? I was so exhausted with the overwhelming anguish, fear and anxiety I was creating in my head that I had to stop the hamster wheel from spinning out of control.

But how?

I grew so tired of feeling anxious, fearful, and emotionless that I felt like I was at rock bottom. I started to really lean into my faith and started focusing more on what I could control. It was an arduous process of getting out of my own head and facing the fears straight on. I had many conversations and pep talks with myself. I had to change the story I was telling myself and create a new one. I would ask myself, is this fear or worry valid or controllable? If not I must learn to let go. I spent too much of my life worrying and obsessing about things that I truly had no reason to worry about. I recall my Dad saying many times to me growing up, what is the point in worrying? He half kiddingly would say, "You could walk outside and get hit by a bus tomorrow."

I wasted precious time and energy that I will never retrieve. It's as if I was the passenger of a plane I was not flying. No matter how much useless energy I spent on trying to control situations, ultimately I was not in the driver's seat. I don't want you to make the same mistake. We will talk more in the upcoming chapters on how to change the nagging, poisonous voices in your head.

Chapter 6

Surrendering To What I Can't Control

"I surrender. I will trust
your plan for my life."
- Matthew 6 31-34

I found that I needed to accept that life won't be the way I had envisioned. My story may not be your story but we relate to pieces of each others' in our own way. We may see ourselves in each other. I share my journey not to make you sad or make you feel pity for me, but the opposite. I want you to find happiness and inspiration knowing that if a woman who experienced such devastating loss at a young age can find purpose through pain, so can you.

Here I am in my late forties and I finally feel like I am fairly equipped to handle many of life's challenges after surviving so much. I know without a doubt because of my faith, that these trials led to the slow evolution of my mission. So many people admire my strength and ask how I got to this point. Let me first say, it was quite the journey and I wouldn't wish this on anyone! I never envisioned my life would be such a tumultuous ride. Moving forward, I am not guaranteed an easy or pain free life and nobody ever is. There are no future guarantees that I won't be faced with more struggles, but I am wiser and feel more equipped to handle the battles of life and coach others.

Just like a shower slowly gets colder over a period of time, time will slowly heal our hearts. The coldness in our soul will be replaced by warm memories of fondness and love. We will never replace what we have lost, however we will fill the void with other happiness and blessings and learn to live with the wound of our own personal wars and losses.

So many grieving people ask these questions. How long will I feel this way? Will the pain ever dull? How am I going to continue to live knowing my heart is in such pieces? I am here to tell you there are no right or wrong answers to these questions because the journey of healing is different for everyone.

Who are we to decide how long someone can sit in their pool of grief and sorrow? I always tell my children you never know what the person next to you is going through, so never assume anything! That person could be experiencing the worst time of their life and we are making assumptions and judging them on a few minutes of time. Not many people knew how much sadness and heaviness I was carrying on my heart because I was so good at masking it. I could turn on the happy smile and the "no care in the world" type of attitude but deep down my soul was hurting so badly.

So, if you are a friend or family member holding a grieving loved one's hand, just be there. No words are needed. Sometimes silence and your presence is all they need. Personally I found that the minutes, hours, days, months and even years seemed to be clouded together for so long. As if the clock kept turning, the calendar kept being flipped, but my time stood still.

I do know that although it is okay and natural to grieve our entire lives, it is not healthy to drown in our pool of sadness. At some point we have to pick ourselves up and carry our cross. Many times I think of Mother Mary holding infant Jesus and compare my life to hers. Our sons were on borrowed times but they changed the world. I know you may be thinking how am I possibly making this comparison but I believe Steven was placed in my life for purpose just as Jesus served a much bigger one in his life. I actually have

a picture on my wall of Mary holding baby Jesus placed next to a picture of me cradling my baby in my arms knowing he was on a watch. I reflect on the quote by mother Teresa, "Pain and suffering have come into your life, but remember pain, sorrow, suffering are but the kiss of Jesus - a sign that you have come so close to Him that he can kiss you."

I encourage my readers to fill the sadness with a greater purpose to their pain. It may take some time to identify what that purpose may be, but I promise if you dig deep enough and allow yourself to "go there" you will find it. Reflect on what sets your soul on fire,creates passion and where your talents lie and there you will find your WHY. Once you do I encourage you to let it fuel your life. Pour all of your grief into living it. For me I found through servant leadership and helping others that have gone through terrible times that I am living out what God has intended. I truly believe Steven is proud of how I have led others through the darkness to see there is in fact still much light.

Let me share with you my unofficial thought-process that brought me to this place of acceptance and ultimately how my tears of pain led to victory. My hope is that through my journey, you can take the lessons and utilize the tools that helped me. I believe this will propel you forward and not get stuck in the darkness.

I don't really know the exact event or time that my mindset started to shift. I just know that I became so mentally, emotionally, and physically exhausted by the constant worry and fear every single day. Enough was enough. I didn't like who I was. I looked in the mirror and asked myself if this was how I wanted to carry on for the rest of my life. I couldn't continue on the path of thinking I could control what was to happen in life. I had to grab the "bull by its horns" and focus on what I could control in my circle.

I spent countless hours in the shower pooling my tears but eventually it was time to "dry" off and put my big girl pants on. Steven and my Dad would want this for me. I just needed to have this burning desire and give myself the ability to relinquish my suffocating sadness.

I think that was first. I had to let go of the uncontrollable. Oh! There are so many but the biggest fears or stressors in my life are the health of my loved ones and pleasing everyone. Yes for sure I am an empath and want everyone to live in peace. The reality is I can't control the decisions of others and I can't control if people will get sick. I had to trust in God that what was to be would be. I dug into my faith.

My faith was rattled to the core so many times that I needed to find what that meant for me. Growing up in a fairly strict Catholic environment and attending Catholic school for 16 years you would think I wouldn't vacillate in my religious beliefs. When I was told Steven was going to die before the age of one I was angry to say the least. How could my God forsake me and allow me to watch my baby suffer? Many times I would set foot in the shower and barter with him. If he just healed my son he could take me instead. Clearly God had other plans and I had to trust in that greater plan. The night before Steven passed, I had asked the local priest to come give Steven his last rites as we knew it was only a matter of time. I felt so angry that a man under God's law couldn't offer any peace. He went through the process emotionless as if it were a menial task and offered no comfort or hope to us.

It took me a long time to find that trust and confidence in our religion again. Who am I to decide that this shouldn't be my life? Why did he choose this for me and my family? So many questions, and when I exited the shower, the answers didn't come for a long time. Perhaps because I didn't want to hear them, I wasn't listening, or I wasn't ready to open up. I needed to relinquish the control to God. Faith is choosing to let go of our need to control and trust that there is a plan much bigger than we know. Without faith in tough times, it is nearly impossible to have hope.

I believe in the power of prayer and I am grateful for my faith. My Faith, although it was shook to the very core, is something I relied on heavily to pull me from the abyss. Faith is the belief that goodness exists despite all of the sorrow. Faith is taking the tiniest little seed and trusting that with proper nourishment from our soul it will sprout into a beautiful flower. This idea is included in Matthew 17:20 "He replied, 'Because you have so little faith, Truly I tell you, if you have faith as small as a mustard seed, you can say to this mountain. Move from here to there, and it will move. Nothing will be impossible for you." You see, just the littlest amount of trust in God can grow, and the more you lean in, your blessings will flourish. Out of the smallest of things, the biggest joys can abound!

I learned to pray, not only during the dark times for God to pull me through, but also through the glorious times, praising him for all of the many blessings I do have in life. I encourage you to converse with our highest being and to trust and seek the light when the darkness seems endless. If you don't give in, I promise the light will slowly win over the dark.

Another factor I needed to be aware of was spending too much time getting lost in what Steven would look like, how would he interact with his siblings, what sports would he be playing, where would he go to college. It is so hard to not imagine all the what ifs. Most people are not aware of all these feelings as their child who is the same age as Steven would be, go about their life. Yes, comparison is the thief of joy. I have to constantly rein back in - all of the "what ifs", "could have beens", or "should have beens."

My father wrote this poem that sums up all of the hopes and dreams that were shattered...

To never know
The grip of his tiny hand
As we walk along a
Path

The sound of his giggle
The kick of the water's splash
When he takes a bath.

Telling funny stories
Silly jokes, a jolly
Song
Phrases with no meaning
No rhymes that
Belong.
The bounce of a ball
In a game of
Catch
The tumbles & falls
Healing kisses to a bruise
A bump or a
Scratch.
To marvel at his growing tall
To his toiling at his
Sport.
The winning, the losing
The rivals he would thwart.

When he discovers a dream
And finds his first
Love
Blinded by his feelings,
Never know nor thought of.

The man
Grown more serious with time
Crafted by its passage
Journeys through life's valleys
Taking on his

Hill.
Tolling in his field
Harvesting his fruits
Loving the challenge,
The game and its
Thrill
No- I will never know
But in truth I will
Tho the time was too short
The break too
Un-even
But my mind will mend all
Thank God for the memory
The memory of
Steven.

I also learned that it was okay to talk about my sadness and grief and allow others to help. This was difficult because I never wanted to play the victim or be portrayed as weak. As time has passed I realized that this was a part of the healing process. We need to allow people into our story. I always say, "I am just keeping it real" because many people judge what they assume to be the perfect life yet they have no idea what I have endured until I share my story. By sharing our struggles we allow other people to open up and allow their feelings to be validated. So many times, women will thank me for being transparent and vulnerable because it gives them the courage to do the same. They feel like it gets them "unstuck" and able to move forward.

Speaking of moving forward, I find the hardest days after losing a loved one or experiencing tragedy are the anniversary dates-birthdays, holidays, death dates, etc. The first year after Steven passed, the anticipation of these days was dreadful and sorrowful. I pulled myself around like I weighed five hundred pounds. What I have found to be the most helpful though is to plan something in memory of the person who passed or even have some sort of celebration. Yes, this sounds crazy, but how would your loved one want you to carry on? On Steven's birthday each year, we have a cake and talk about him. I write a birthday card and put it in his memory box. We also do something to honor him such as a small fundraiser or making a donation in his memory. I encourage you to celebrate the person who is not physically with you but in every other aspect is present in your heart and mind.

I must mention here that we attach animals, music, objects or places to those we love and to our special memories. Nestle was no exception!

I associated and attached our chocolate lab Nestle (like the chocolate bar) to Steven. He was our first pet together. We got him from a little farm in New Jersey and knew that even though we weren't supposed to have pets in our tiny third floor apartment, we wanted to add him to our family. Nestle was a constant in our crazy life. He sat by Isobel and guarded her crib at night in New Jersey, he laid by the green plush couch that Steven spent the majority of his life on in Maryland, he played with  Blaise in the snow in New York and he greeted Jake happily into the world in Delaware. The day we had to put him down was a dark one for certain. He was faithful through so many life events (the good, the bad and the ugly) and I was so attached to that dog. When he took his last breathe my heart broke just a little more. He was another connection to my son. I knew that pup was licking Steven's face in Heaven though!

Losing My Identity and recreating WHO I AM

You know as you grow up you envision what your life will be? You make all these plans and assume they will go exactly the way you envision. But what happens when our dream becomes shattered? When our life as we had hoped goes way off course? How do we adjust?

How often do you focus on how life should have gone or what could be if only? Many people I have spoken with over the years struggle with this concept the most. We spend so much time preparing for how we want our life to be and controlling every aspect but once something falls apart or doesn't go the way we imagined it would, we crumble.

I think of women or men who have spent several years married and then suddenly their spouse is leaving them with no warning. This is truly traumatic and life altering. The happily ever after turns into creating a new life they never imagined. The parent who lost their child in a car accident and had no time to prepare for life without this child. The soldier who got wounded in battle and has to learn how to walk with one leg. The mom of two who battles Stage 2 breast cancer and has to quit her job because she needs constant chemo and is sick all the time. The woman who desires a child but is not able to conceive. How do we cope with such unexpected horrible situations or life altering events?

I reflect back on John Maxwell's book *The 15 Invaluable Laws of Growth*. One of the chapters, The Law of Pain strikes a cord. He states about devastation, "As unfair,unreasonable, and impossible as it seems,we still have work to do after a tragedy occurs. We still have roles to fill.We still have responsibility to family and others. The stuff of life may pause for a while, but it doesn't stop. Fair or not, that is a reality." Here is the thing - life owes us nothing. Once we accept that, our minds can shift into the possibilities and choices we make based on how triumphant we want to be. The reality for me is that I suffered major losses, but how I choose to react or respond will decide my future - a future without Steven.

I really try not to think about what he would be doing with his life as today he would be 19. I don't expect people to understand or emphasize what it feels like as I watch other young men Steven's age go off to college, play sports, have a girlfriend, or interact with his siblings.

As I write this, the third treatment was recently approved for SMA. I cry tears of joy and sadness in the shower. I am so happy for all those parents who get to see their children receive these treatments and medications that will hopefully stave off the debilitating symptoms of SMA and have a "normal" life, but sad that Steven is not here to have this option. All the grueling hours my family and I put into basket raffles, dinner dances, runs, golf tournaments and so many other fundraisers have paid off! I truly didn't believe in my lifetime I would see so much promise to "cure" this disease but here I am 2021 and Thank God there is not just one, but three treatment options for SMA!

Honestly, I don't go down this road too often. Really what purpose would this serve? Sitting in my shower of tears and pity would not serve me or my family. However, give yourself permission to "daydream" a bit, because it wouldn't be natural if we avoid what it would, could, or should be like.

Let's face it - life would be very different if the person or thing we grieved was here or the situation was different. I spend a lot of time wishing to have a conversation with my father as he was the voice of reason in my life. When I feel this overwhelming sadness I allow it in and then think about how this sorrow has also allowed my purpose to penetrate my being. This pain has brought me exactly where I need to be because I acknowledged it but didn't let it drown me. My pain led me to help so many others to have the "what could have been" become their new reality. Now, don't get me wrong I was submerged holding my breath many times but always lifted my head to open my mouth and exhale. Just breathe!

I know some of the hardest times of pure agony and grief, are the holidays, anniversaries, birthdays and special occasions. The firsts without our loved ones are simply dreaded and horrible. Knowing those days were coming I tended to sulk and feel overwhelming anxiety. I just wanted to get through and move on. As I reflect back, I can't even remember or cherish so many of those special times because I felt so sad and depressed. Then I feel upset because I "missed" out on those special days with the ones present in my life. It is a situation where you feel there is no winning.

So what would my recommendation be to you after living

through it? As I stated earlier, there is no rule book to the right or appropriate ways to grieve. It is truly survival mode, one baby step at a time. Something I would suggest is documenting or journaling the special times with your loved ones. As I reflect back, all I have is pictures from these moments and it pains me to know I can't bring the time back or bring some of the good memories to the forefront of my mind. In addition, have something close to your heart that was meaningful to them or symbolized your love for that person. I wear a heart pendant around my neck with a piece of Steven's hair. I was also gifted a blanket made from special shirts of my father. Whatever is meaningful for you, I encourage you to cherish the little things. It doesn't have to make sense to anyone else!

I lost so much during the sadness. I can't recall my other children's reactions and joy at the holidays instead I recall how I missed Steven and my Dad so much.

Something I have found to be helpful and create happiness is to honor our loved ones on their birthday and on the holidays. For example, we put Steven's stocking up every year and write a note or put a special ornament in it. We donate to hospice each year in his memory.

Christmas was also my Dad's most favorite time of the year. We would shop for my mom and then go to The Pub in Pennsauken, New Jersey the week before Christmas. Even though he was German he identified as an Italian. He cooked the traditional seven fishes and much more every Christmas Eve. My parents would invite several family and friends over to celebrate together. It was truly a magical time. In honor of my Dad, we incorporate one of his traditions into our family meal and always toast him with limoncello. So, continue what you may have done with your angel or create a new memory so you look forward to these times instead of dreading them. Just be patient with yourself.

I don't have all the answers but because I have lived through it, I can suggest ways to not just LIVE and survive, but THRIVE, and find happiness and purpose through the pain. It is a slow, tedious, and painful process, however, it is possible! There is hope despite the heartache we will feel forever. John Maxwell says it best, "If there is hope in the future, there is power in the present."

Acknowledging and walking through the messy difficult heart wrenching feelings and being present with your emotions and feelings are necessary in order to accept and move forward.

Chapter 7

Mentally Stronger Through the
Five Intrinsic (G)ifts

*"You don't have to be great to start,
but you have to start to be great"*
- Zig Ziglar

Over the past few years, I have turned to leaders in the personal growth and development field. I was seeking a better way to live and to not feel frozen all the time. After much soul searching, I slowly started unwrapping my intrinsic gifts that were with me the whole time. I had to be ready to open them and use them to propel my purpose. I just had to start!

Through my five intrinsic gifts of gratitude, generosity, growth, grit and grace, I truly found myself, improved my mindset and became a better human. Let's explore how these gifts can improve your mindset and create a fantastic hopeful future.

Gratitude
*the quality of being thankful;
readiness to show appreciation
for and to return kindness.*

As I step in the shower, I am overcome with gratitude for my many blessings, despite the heartaches I have experienced. I cry tears of joy instead of sorrow, praising God for the goodness he has bestowed upon me. Yes I had to make choices to embrace the goodness as it is simpler to fall into the "poor little old me trap." As Zig Ziglar states, "Gratitude is the healthiest of all emotions. The more we express gratitude for what you have, the more likely you will have even more to express gratitude for." I found this statement to become quite appropriate for my new found mindset.

I focused on those people in my life that I was appreciative of.

After the death of Steven, many friends slowly started distancing themselves. My involvement with Cure SMA however, led me to new friendships that still exist to this very day. You have heard the saying when one door closes a new one opens and that is very true for friendships as well. Reflect back on a time in your life when you went through a rough patch. Ask yourself who were the people who stood by your side? They might have been tough on you and told you what you needed to hear, instead of what you wanted to hear,but they were loyal to you. I encourage you to find a tribe that lifts you up, makes you a better person and expects nothing less of you.

I focused on the blessing of my amazing support network. Our families stood by us, supported every fundraising event and gave us the encouragement needed to continue to find happiness. They have been our biggest cheerleaders throughout the many storms we have encountered.

My husband Jason to this day is my anchor to my rocking boat. He is my person that listens without judgement and just holds me up when all I want to do is collapse. Many times throughout our years of marriage we struggled. There were months at a time that we didn't know if we were going to make it. We reminded each other of the hurt we constantly lugged around. I believe what has carried us through and made our marriage more resilient is an understanding that we both hurt.

I focused on my God-given gifts. For example, I started teaching fitness classes in local gyms and started connecting with people again. For so long, I felt isolated from the real world and when I found my passion for fitness and inspiring others to live more healthy, I felt such a sense of gratitude and appreciation of my talents. Movement through music was one of my talents. I found such comfort turning up the tunes and being carefree. Try it! I promise you will automatically feel better when you jam out to your favorite beats!

I embraced the idea of starting and ending each day with three things I was grateful for. Now it had to be specific such as, I am thankful my husband brought me coffee or I appreciate the kind gesture of someone smiling today or holding the door. When we focus on gratitude, it is hard to be hateful. It's the little things in life that truly add up. As Zig Ziglar says, "The greatest source of happiness is the ability to be grateful at all times."

I encourage you to do this every day. After a week of expressing gratitude, pay attention to how your mindset changes. We tend to shift our perspective on life when we move away from the negativity and focus on all of the positive aspects in our life. When you shift your mind to your blessings the health benefits are amazing including:

1. Improved sleep
2. Lower heart rate
3. Improved relationships
4. Lower stress (cortisol) levels
5. Increase in energy
6. Reduced anxiety/depression
7. Increased productivity

Growth
*the process of developing or maturing
physically, mentally, or spiritually.*

I learned that pushing myself out of my comfort zone was the only way Growth would happen. I felt stuck and frozen for so many years. I was wrapped up in my own web and couldn't escape. I truly lost my identity over the years and had to rediscover who I was and what all of this meant for me. As Wayne Dyer states, "If you change the way you look at things, the things you look at change." I had to make the choice to pull myself up from all of the weight that was truly holding me down. It was truly time to grow onward and upward. I decided to view everything through bright lenses instead of dark ones.

As a younger woman, I didn't listen to motivational speakers. I wasn't familiar the names such as Zig Ziglar, Jim Rohn, Tony Robbins, John Maxwell, Brene Brown, Mel Robbins, Maya Angelou, or Les Brown - just to name a few. At some point in 2017, a popup on the computer came up with an advertisement about John Maxwell. I started listening to his words of wisdom and found a profound calling to find out more about coaching, training, and this certification program. I knew it was time for a change in my life but at that point I honestly didn't know where it was coming from. After speaking with a member of his team, I truly took a leap of faith and signed up for the certification.

I had a yearning deep down to serve others but I didn't have all of the tools I needed. Attending John's event was transformative. I was so outside of my comfort zone but I was in the right place! The 2000 people in the room were there for the same reason. They had all experienced significant trials in their life but they wanted to grow personally so they could serve others. John Maxwell said, "Success is when I add value to myself. Significance is when I add value to others." I wanted to be this person! I was humbled by this experience and knew that my life was going to change for the better!

After I attended John Maxwell Training, I continued on my growth journey and invested in myself. I was so drawn to a man named Zig Ziglar. (Yes sounds like a cartoon character). He was one of the most well known and respected motivational and  inspiring speakers in the world! I was inspired by so many of his quotes that I decided to attend the Ziglar Legacy Training in Dallas, Texas. Again, forcing myself outside of my comfy little box. As I stood in shower the night before I was to attend the Ziglar legacy Certification, a wave of emotion coursed through me. This time the feelings were of nervous excitement and joy! I knew there was a reason I needed to go and that another life-changing weekend was in store. My biggest takeaway from this training was - what legacy do I want to leave my children and those that I love? Tom Ziglar, Zig's son and CEO of Ziglar, Inc. says, "Legacy is intentionally preparing those you love to grow through life's most difficult challenges." Wow! Up until this point I thought legacy was what material possessions I would leave behind. Now my viewpoint on what I want to leave behind shifted. My attitude, efforts, actions, despite the trials and tribulations of life, will leave a lasting impression on those I love. This aspect is so critical especially during trying times. Our children and everyone around us will be watching how we respond.

There are so many ways to add growth to your life that may not cost a thing. Be curious, ask questions, do not settle for what seems to be, but instead ask why, what if. You could listen to podcasts that interest you on topics you enjoy. You can spend time with a mentor, someone you look up to and admire. You can take a class on something you have always wanted to learn, read an inspiring book, participate in an activity with a group of people you don't know. How about doing something you fear but you've always wanted to try? The point is to be uncomfortable! You will never regret growth!

Generosity
the quality of being kind and generous.

I grew up with very generous, selfless parents. They helped anyone in need and were always the first to offer assistance. I know my sense of a giving heart came from them. To me, generosity is the abundance of love and the blessings of our time bestowed to others. It is giving your most treasured talents and gifts to help others in their life's journey. I have given thousands of hours of my time and talents to so many!

Because of my community involvement, I was recognized as a leader and given a once in a lifetime opportunity to serve as an honorary commander at The Dover Air Force Base for three years. This was quite a distinction because I experienced the missions of our military in a way that most people could never imagine. I flew in the cockpit of a C-5 (the United States Air Force's largest military transport aircraft) during a combat landing and witnessed a mid air refueling. I toured Cheyenne Mountain in Colorado, a top secret installation where NORAD, North American Aerospace Defense Command, is located. I was paired with the Commander of Joint Personal Effects Department, where the mission is "to receive, safeguard, inventory, store, process, and determine the final disposition of personal effects of not only those killed in action, but also those who are wounded or missing from all branches of the military."

I share these experiences because we never know what is in store for us when we lead with a generous heart. I encourage you to find something in your life that you feel so passionate about that you pour your heart and soul into it with no expectations other than filling up your own cup. I truly believe a giving heart will receive 100x over what it bestowed.

To this day I continue to run the local chapter of Cure SMA. I am so proud of combined efforts of many that we have brought in close to 2.5 million dollars for research. This organization now has three effective treatments and I feel there is a cure coming soon. Wow! All I wanted to see in my lifetime was this! In addition to fundraising, my husband and I met with many parents who sadly were going through similar journeys as ours and needed just a hand to hold or an ear to listen. They looked to us as a beacon of hope in such a hopeless time in their life. I can recall many conversations where I didn't have the words they needed but I could offer them a hand to hold or a shoulder to cry on.

I would donate tons of profits from classes and workshops as well as lead events for many local charities. I even participated in the local Dancing with the Delaware Stars to benefit charities nine times! I used my gifts of connecting to others and my passion of wellness to give back to the community. Zig Ziglar says, "You can have everything in life you want if you will just help enough other people get what they want."

I pour my heart and soul into listening and supporting other women who are going through very tough situations in their life. I encourage them to find what makes them happy and fulfill their aspirations. If my journey of pain and healing can help anyone then my purpose is being fulfilled. Take some time and reflect on your talents, your God given abilities that can add value to others. We all have them! Think about what makes your heart sing, brings you joy and lights up your soul.

Grit
In psychology, grit is a positive, non-cognitive trait based on an individual's perseverance of effort combined with the passion for a particular long-term goal or end state.

I absolutely love this word! Through all of my challenges I had to dig deep and not give in to the doubts and fears that crossed my mind daily. When I think of this word it ignites a fire deep in my soul! People with grit dig in when times are tough, are resilient in any situation,unbreakable and push through the darkness to see the light!

Some believe you are born with grit. You either have it or you don't. But I don't buy into that mindset. You can develop toughness. I reflect on a quote by Nassim Taleb in his book *AntiFragile: Things That Gain From Disorder* where he states that being Antifragile is, "a property of systems that increase in capability, resilience, robustness as a result of stressors, shocks, volatility, noise, mistakes, faults, attacks or failures." You see, we have a choice to make on how we will respond to every situation in life. You can choose to succumb to the hardships or dig in, be resilient and antifragile. This is a beautiful freedom. We get to make that call.

As an avid athlete, grit has brought me through to some of my prouder moments. As author Angela Duckworth states in her book *Grit: The Power of Passion and Perseverance*, "Grit is living life like a marathon and not a sprint." I reflect back to the time I signed up for the Marine Corps Marathon as my first way to really acknowledge what Steven battled in just a small way and to raise awareness for Spinal Muscular Atrophy. I trained for about four months to prepare my body for the 26.2 mile course that would lead me to the finish line. I thought I was prepared for this day! I had major butterflies that morning in October as I stood at the starting line with thousands of others. It was such a humbling moment looking around as everyone there participated for their own reasons and purpose. Fortunately, my husband was my running buddy so I was confident we wouldn't let each other down. As each mile passed my legs and feet started to ache and feel so heavy.

My shoulders ached from the tension and worse the mind started playing tricks and telling me negative talk. I believe we are capable of whatever our mind tells us to do. Yes grit was the only way I would cross the line. I shifted the talk in my head and literally just put one foot in front of the other and finished the race!

I think we all agree there is no better feeling, than the sense of accomplishment when we achieve what we set out to do!

Another event I participated in reminds me of how I depended on bringing out my fierceness and bravery. I was invited to participate in a relay called American Odyssey. This is a 12-person relay race that runs from Gettysburg, PA to Washington D.C. Running long distances is not too challenging for me, but facing some other fears such as running the cemetery battlegrounds at two in the morning, well that was terrifying. I knew this would be a test of my fears and I faced it head on. Did I mention it was storming and yes thunder and lightning terrify me as well? But how will we ever grow and learn if we don't push outside of our safe haven? Fear truly holds us back from living a fulfilled life. I challenge you to face a fear and just do it! You will be incredibly proud and it will propel you to go even farther than you ever imagined.

What is one fear you have that you would like to overcome? Or what is a situation that you need to use grit to get through? Or what is something you can plan to participate in that will challenge you mentally and physically?

Grace
unmerited divine assistance given to
humans for their regeneration or
sanctification or a virtue coming from God

Last but certainly not least is grace. This word is significant, and an essential element of Christianity.

"My grace is sufficient for you, for my power is made perfect in weakness." - 2 Corinthians 12:9

God offers us unending grace, forgiveness and love when we need it the most. Grace is acknowledging there will be times in our life where we may fail, fall short from the goal, make mistakes, and stumble. But how we respond will make all the difference in our mindset. Failure is not a bad word unless you do not learn from it.

Grace is also acknowledging there will be pain and hurt in your life not only brought on by your experiences, but feeling like other people have caused great pain in your life as well. Are we willing to forgive and move past the pain or do we hold onto the anger and resentment? If so, how is that serving your thoughts? I will answer, it is not. These feelings do not serve us and can potentially lead to mental and physical illness.

In addition I like to incorporate "practicing the pause." When a situation arises that upsets or angers you, I encourage you to take a few minutes to breathe and pause before you react. You can practice grace by being intentional, allowing yourself to have bad days and forgiving yourself and others.

Lastly I will add that grace is not comparing yourself to others. Have you ever heard the quote by Theodore Roosevelt, "Comparison is the thief of joy?" Well, this my friend, is true. Walk in your shoes and live your own unique life. The reality is, only you can own and write your story.

How can you incorporate grace into your life now? Is there something you are holding on to that is holding you back from living your best life?

Sometimes just showing up is a win all unto itself. Getting out of bed, brushing your teeth, making a meal, getting dressed, driving your kids to school, you get the picture. It can be a challenge after you have experienced great loss. Many times during the past 19 years, I have allowed the word grace to step in and save me. I admit I have self-medicated on and off for many years, not with any illegal drugs, but things that were just suppressing my reality. Let me settle on this for a moment and be honest; not once during all of these years did I allow myself to fall into addictive habits.

However, many that experience such trauma are tempted to escape reality. And, I get it. In fact, more often than not, survivors of trauma tend to start finding ways to mask the pain in unhealthy ways. If this is you, I encourage you to seek professional help or at the very least reach out to someone like myself who understands and can support you on the journey to recovery.

Chapter 8

"Do not conform to the pattern of this world,
but be transformed by the renewing of your mind.
Then you will be able to test and approve what
God's will is-his good, pleasing and perfect will."
-Romans 12:2

It seems so ironic to say we can find blessings through loss and allow changes to occur that can lead to a true transformation. As I reflect back on the years of survival, I was planting the seeds of positive transfiguration all along my way.

Even though, at the time, I didn't think I was making a difference now I can see how my path to healing led to beautiful blooms for not only myself, but for others as well. I know the death of Steven not only led to beautiful changes in my life but saved others in some ways. We never know whose life we may change by just caring.

The beauty of loss is that we never know where it will lead us. We may feel adrift for so long but when we pour into others despite our pain, we create a change that can ripple!

Below are a few stories of how the impact of this little baby could affect others that he never met. Because of Steven and the values my Dad instilled in me, I was privileged to truly serve others.

My work in leading the chapter led to beautiful encounters with other families and children affected by this disease. I was able to help families purchase handicapped accessible vans and equipment. Because this disease is so variable, it is not easy or inexpensive to secure these items. Our chapter supported the purchase of a service dog for a teenager. We have witnessed kids and adults become stronger through the approved treatments. I have watched SMA kids grow up to become amazing young adults serving their community and living out their dreams despite their "handicap." I have developed life long friendships and attended weddings and parties of those who I met because of Steven.

I feel so proud of the choices I made. Despite my sorrow I was somehow able to put it aside to serve. A few years ago when I was part of the honorary commander program that I mentioned, I presented to a group of service members. As I nervously stood in front of the men and women serving our country, I doubted how my story could benefit them. How wrong I was. After I finished speaking, a gentleman came up to me with tears in his eyes and thanked me for being so authentic and vulnerable. He then shared with me that his adult cousin suffered many debilitating diseases that left him unable to walk. This marine's dream was to have his cousin ride a bike with him through the streets of Philadelphia.

After listening to him, I knew immediately I would help him fulfill this dream. Within a few weeks I supported him getting a fundraising page set up to purchase a handicapped accessible bike to pull his cousin behind. Through the work with another non-profit Ainsley's Angels, he raised more than enough to fulfill his mission. Within months his cousin was enjoying the beautiful sunshine and many trails! I share this because we never know how we can impact a life simply by listening and offering some time and energy. It is in our darkest hours that lifting others may be what we need to also lift us.

Mental Transformation through loss

Going through the motions of life, I didn't give much thought to my mindset. I honestly didn't know any difference for so long. If you told me twenty years ago that our mindset can dictate our success in life despite horrible setbacks I probably would have dismissed that idea rather quickly. I wasn't taught this in school and I never had a reason to give much thought to how our beliefs could shape our future. I literally was along for the ride instead of creating the ride! However, within the past few years the "Aha!" moments started coming to me because I sought out change! I wanted more out of life than just getting by and staying on the same merry go round.

Indeed, just like we can strengthen and change our bodies through effort, we can also grow our brains. Okay, but how? According to Carol Dweck, a famous Professor of Psychology, she explains the difference of a fixed versus growth mindset.

A "fixed mindset" assumes that our character, intelligence, and creative ability are static givens which we can't change in any meaningful way, and success is the affirmation of that inherent intelligence, an assessment of how those givens measure up against an equally fixed standard; striving for success and avoiding failure at all costs become a way of maintaining the sense of being smart or skilled.

A "growth mindset," on the other hand, thrives on challenge and sees failure not as evidence of unintelligence but as a heartening springboard for growth and for stretching our existing abilities. Out of these two mindsets, which we manifest from a very early age, springs a great deal of our behavior, our relationship with success and failure in both professional and personal contexts, and ultimately our capacity for happiness.

Source:
https://www.brainpickings.org/2014/01/29/carol-dweck-mindset/

I began to ask the question what does this really mean? In a nutshell, we decide whether we will allow challenges to keep us stuck in the same pattern of life or instead propel us to make a difference and grow from the setbacks. We had to get to the point that we are so uncomfortable with who we are, that we are forced to grow and change. Sometimes we have to get to the lowest points in life in order to recognize we need a personal revolution. Ultimately, our mental decisions create the blueprint for our life.

I chose to adopt the growth mindset when I knew that what I was thinking, believing and doing was negatively affecting me in every way and I felt I was at rock bottom.

This mental process led to transformation.

Change versus Transformation

I believe change is inevitable and transformation is a choice. Changes happen every day all around and in us. Just like all of you, I have had thousands of changes in my life.

Besides the obvious losses- my kids becoming young adults, my husband joining the military again, new friendships, hormonal and health changes, the list goes on.

However, these changes don't lead to anything lasting or worthwhile unless we apply positive thoughts, emotions and behaviors consistently to what it means for our life. A true metamorphosis will occur when you walk the difficult roads, allow the tears to flow but continue to press on until you reach the desired outcome.

My own transformation happened when I invested in me after neglecting myself for many years. I ignored all the warning signs that were screaming, "you are self destructing!" Yes, I was getting by, I was showing up as a good wife and mom, I was serving others but I was falling apart from the inside. I was the only one who could put the necessary work in to truly transform my mindset that would ultimately lead me to the amazing life I have today.

The definition of triumph to me is victory or success through the metamorphosis of life. "We delight in the beauty of a butterfly but rarely admit the changes it has gone through to achieve that beauty" states Maya Angelou, a well-known poet, civil rights activist and memoirist. Despite how tough the journey was, I chose to embrace the changes in order to create a magnificent transformation.

I am proud of the woman I am today. The road was not easy as I faced many difficulties and setbacks. However, I made the decisions along the path that led me to what I consider now to be a successful life. I believe the one quality that led to my transformation is RESILIENCE.

Chapter 9

The Power of Resilience

*"I can be changed by what happens
to me but I refuse to be reduced by it"
- Maya Angelou*

Those 5 G's of Gifts of Gratitude, Generosity, Growth, Grit and Grace definitely helped define my purpose and become mentally stronger but there is much more that goes into being resilient or "bouncing back" after a terrible loss. Throughout the past nineteen years I have spent a lot of time reflecting on how I was able to not just survive all of the grief but truly thrive and find peace and happiness again. After all, many people do not come through as well as others.

How do we prepare to go through life's most difficult challenges and flourish? I have come to the conclusion that there are many ways to navigate and every individual sails differently through the storms of life. Some people barely hold on for dear life, and others seem to simply glide effortlessly without skipping a beat. What sets the survivors and thrivers apart?

Ultimately

Our mindset! We determine our mental toughness, therefore, how we are to live our lives. This is not something you can teach but instead you learn as you go. The positive power within us is infinite, but you must allow this power to be unleashed in order to free your mind from negativity. Some people seem to be wired strongly from birth but others seem inherently weak. How do we become tougher? I believe that our experiences make us tougher and more resilient.

The word **RESILIENCE**. Let me break down what this word truly means to me and how we can apply it to our lives in the arduous times.

R (Rubber bandish) Think of the point of a rubber band. It is created to stretch under tension to hold something together. This is life. We must be flexible and learn to stretch outside of our comfort zones in order to grow and succeed despite the daily pressures. In times of grief, we may act like a rubber band, putting ourselves under pressure during those difficult days to just get by. We may not like this uncomfortable feeling but we can choose to tolerate it until it becomes less "painful" then we can stretch even more.

E (Energy) Energy creates movement and momentum. The more you get moving the easier it becomes to keep going. Energy creates excitement. How do you create energy though? Energy is sparked by purpose! Think of your most successful, enjoyable days in life. You have a purpose that day, whether it's presenting a project at work, preparing for a birthday party or packing for a trip. All of these have a purpose! Where our focus goes, our energy goes. I encourage you to have a daily purposes to create energy and focus!

S (Self Aware) Knowing who you are, what you stand for and taking responsibility and ownership of our actions creates resilience.We don't make excuses for the person we are, shaped by our experiences yet we can hone in on our strengths and acknowledge our weaknesses.

I (Intentional) Being intentional means our actions are executed with purpose.This is something I talk to my children about often. When we make choices in life with deliberate purpose then we usually don't have regret because they are well thought out and desire a specific outcome.

L (Love) In order to be resilient you must love yourself first. In times of hardships we may miss the mark on infinite self love and self care because we are in such deep pain and despair. I encourage you to focus on your well being including what we discussed in the previous chapter.

I (Indestructible) No matter what is thrown at us in life, we will persevere and not destruct or break! When we experience loss it is easy to crack and self destruct. However if we are resilient we allow the darkness to settle in knowing full well that the light is not far off. We just need to seek it out and be patient.

E (Evolving) Our lives are constant, and nothing stays the same even if we want it to. We must allow flexibility into our life, knowing the ebbs and flows are always present. The most successful people acknowledge and push through discomfort in order to move on to the next step, the next goal, the next dream.

N (Nourishing) When we contribute positive information, nutritious food, quality sleep, and purposeful movement into our life ultimately we are setting ourselves up for success. When we recognize that something or someone is unhealthy how do we nurse it back to health? We focus on the areas of weakness,illness or devastation and we gently but firmly guide it to a better place. We nourish it with whatever it needs or is depleted of.

C (Capable) This is the belief in ourselves that we can accomplish anything we set our minds to despite the setbacks, sadness or failures we have experienced. We develop the qualities it takes to achieve what we know is possible. This book was something I dreamed of writing for a long time but I had to believe in myself that I could do it. Once the belief was instilled in me, I set up a plan to execute and deliver. Nothing can be accomplished without having a plan in place and we need to have faith in our competency.

E (Empathy) Perhaps one of hardest parts of grief and loss is being able to understand what that person is experiencing. I spoke earlier on how insensitive some people seemed perhaps because they lacked empathy or were truly scared away from my emotions. By offering empathy we can put ourselves in others shoes and simply acknowledge their pain. Offer an ear to listen, a shoulder to cry on or a hand to hold. Just the simple act of being present may be enough.

I contribute my toughness and resilience to activities and experiences throughout my years. I think back to when I was a tiny eight year old competitive gymnast standing on the 4 inch wide balance beam preparing to do two backflips. Even at that young age, I had to rely on my mental strategy and convince myself I was capable and brave! I could convince myself I would get injured and fail or I could visualize success and just go for it! Another flashback is standing at the start line of a Cross Country race in high school. My thoughts contributed to my success or failure depending on what I focused on. If I visualized running my best race and not paying attention to distractions I was more apt to succeed!

Mental toughness can be compared to building your physical strength. The only way to become stronger and build bigger muscles is to keep at it. You persevere, you add weights, you tear down to build up. I think of an egg in its natural fragile state - easily breakable, and weak to touch. However, if you put that egg in boiling water it becomes stronger, more resilient. We are the egg. Inherently weak but put under pressure we will become tougher if we don't break. Again, the word antifragile comes to mind as I think about resiliency.

Wow! This is exactly how we move through life's most difficult heartbreaks, failures, losses, and challenges. We persevere through the heartbreaks of life, and we become antifragile. If we take the pain (no one escapes from this) and use it to create purpose, then we are building our legacy muscles.

Pain changes us for better or for worse. As John Maxwell says, "Pain prompts us to face who we are and where we are. What we do with the experience defines who we are." In my opinion, loss is the worst pain known to humans. We can not replace what has gone, but we can learn from it, grow from it and change from it. As Virginia Satir, an author and therapist says, "Life is not the way it's supposed to be. It's the way it is. The way you cope with it is what makes the difference." This is our choice. I decided I want to live and love and not drown in sadness. I made the decision to not be the victim but instead become the victor. After all is said and done, I want to leave a legacy for those I love that despite the hardships in my life, I persevered and chose joy and purpose instead of despair and sadness.

Chapter 10

Self-Care from Grief to Healing

"Prioritizing self care is a crucial part of the healing process. When we are not well for ourselves, we are unfit to serve others."
-Jessica Moyer

As part of my journey from pain to purpose I have made it part of my mission to promote wellness and self care. As we experience grief and loss we tend to forget about self care and then we may spend years playing catch up to become physically,mentally, emotionally and spiritually healthy. As I had previously mentioned I lived through two very different health scenarios - Steven did not get a choice in his life about how to take care of his health and on the other hand my father chose everyone else's health over his own.

This has propelled me to preach the importance of caring for yourself first. When we go into battles in our life, the only way we will survive and thrive and help others to fight is to put on our armor first.

Think about a time in your life when you were ill. Were you able to care for everyone who depends on you? Were you able to perform your daily activities at all and if so to what extent? How about in the times of grief, when you are mentally so worn down but your body still has to show up?

I truly believe the reason my mom suffered a massive stroke was partly due to the overwhelming grief of missing my dad, but also because she was neglecting her health and ignoring the warning signals. It is proven that when we are under extreme or prolonged times of stress, our cortisol levels will elevate. If you stay at this high rate of these stress hormones, your mind and body will start to break down in some way. It is just a matter of time.

In May of 2019, I opened a boutique wellness studio in my community to promote this mission. Honestly, it happened very organically. I worked in so many fitness facilities, over fifty-five communities, cancer support groups and many more, that I felt it was time to bring everything under one roof. I grew tired of running everywhere to promote my mission and put faith that this was my next calling. I witnessed so many women struggling to find who they were, struggling to incorporate self care in their very busy, overwhelming lives and recognize their worthiness despite enduring tough times.

My space is a welcome and intimate environment for women to come together who have all been through challenging times in life and want to better themselves. I consider this environment such a blessing because I am able to share my story and allow other women to feel vulnerable yet safe. Yes, we workout in  a variety of ways but more importantly we discuss how our mindset can affect our lifestyle. I have witnessed transformations of many women because they were willing to dig deep, acknowledge the "baggage" they are carrying with them and then put in the effort and work it takes to live healthier and more purposeful. Today, I am proud of this community I have built, and I believe this was one of my purposes all along. So, what are some ways that you can manage grief in a healthy way?

Let me emphasize that I know it is difficult to focus on your well being when your sadness and grief is crippling. However, the following suggestions can lift you during these times and maybe make life a little more bearable until the heaviness starts to dissipate. It truly is a choice, but I encourage you to implement some or all of the following:

1. Control the input

We are bombarded with millions of thoughts, beliefs, words, media influx and more every second. How do we decipher the input that matters most, that is true, beneficial and will create positivity and purpose in our world? One of my Ziglar classmates compared our mind to our garden. The seeds we are planting in our garden can become weeds and die or sprout into beautiful flowers depending on how we tend to the growth. If we nurture our garden (mind) with positivity and sunlight imagine the beautiful flowers that will bloom. So I encourage you to be mindful of what you are allowing yourself to be exposed to.

That being said there are times when our mind goes way off course leading to negative thoughts. When the negative sabotaging thoughts start to seep in, you acknowledge then halt them. Automatically replace them with a positive affirmation or thought. I like to think of our thoughts as our imaginary toolbox that can build our world up or tear it down based on what "tools" we choose to use. Thoughts or "our tools" control our emotions. Our emotions are dictated by our very brain, which in turn creates actions. When we are grieving it is very difficult to discern the truth from the "evil." This is a conscious effort. I personally struggle with this every day.

For example, I tend to fixate on health issues. My thoughts tend to drift towards worrying about the little things becoming catastrophic. My son may have a rash and automatically it is cancer in my mind. To counter this, first, I acknowledge yes he has a rash. I keep an eye on it, treat it with medications and focus on what I know to be true. If it's worse then I deal with it when the time comes. Countless times I have made myself sick thinking of the worst case scenario. We are all guilty of it. So instead focus on what you know to be true in that moment. Remember, "what we feed our mind determines our appetite."- Tom Ziglar

The health benefits of positive thinking are numerous. According to The Mayo Clinic you can have decreased rates of depression, lower levels of stress, lower chances of becoming ill, increased psychological and physical well being, more restful sleep just to name a few.

2. Move your body

As I mentioned above, running was my way to work through all of the emotions in my own way and in my time. Have you ever worked out, gone for a walk, taken a bike ride, gone for a hike, played kickball with your child and regretted it? Movement can be an expression of emotions. I find the best way to clear my mind is to dance, run, walk or lift weights-you get the picture. Find an enjoyable activity that requires movement and commit to it! I have personally witnessed many transformations of women experiencing severe depression,sadness or anxiety when they engage in some sort of physical activity. The benefits can include- a release of endorphins, which are feel good hormones in our body; offers a distraction for a period of time; promotes a healthier body; gives us a sense of accomplishment; reduces stress and promotes a sense of community.

3. Have a schedule/plan activities

Have you heard a ship without a destination goes nowhere? Well that is true for our life. If we do not have a plan to follow daily we will spend our time endlessly moping around without a clear sense of direction. After Steven passed, I had to force myself to plan meals, workouts and a fun activity each day with my daughter.

Even if I did not feel like doing it, I realized the importance of keeping a schedule for her and it gave me something to focus on. When we have time on our hands we tend to allow all of the sadness and grief to sit on our hearts and mind. Again, I will reiterate that I know this is easier said than executed and some days you will feel like doing nothing! However, setting yourself on a routine including meals, work, fun time, sleep and down time will help take your mind off that elephant in the room even if for a little while.

If I had only known the importance of these words eighteen years ago. Of course I always prayed and had many conversations or "Come to Jesus" talks, but I thought meditation was for hippies and had no idea really what this word meant. I have come to realize the essence of what it is and find that this word means something different for everyone. I use an app called Calm and some of the guided meditations are specific to grief.

The app states the importance of quiet mindfulness, "When we practice meditation for grieving, we allow ourselves to sit with what we are feeling, even if that feeling is numbness. We create a healthy environment for our pain and emotions to rise to the surface, and what can follow is something magical - a cathartic release of emotion that leads to healing." I have experienced by quieting my mind and getting in touch with my thoughts, emotions and body on a very earthly level leads to a release of pent up toxic feelings.

For example, when I find myself getting riled up or anxious about something, I will stop myself. I hone in on what my thoughts are focusing on and talk myself through a sensible solution or plan. When I coach women we talk about this often. Life can get so deep and exhausting if you allow it. Sometimes stepping away from our immediate reactions can benefit us in multiple ways. Think of a situation in your life when you reacted based on your immediate thoughts and emotions. Did it benefit you or did it backfire on you? This is a very conscious decision you must make in the heat of the moment.

I encourage you to practice the following in times of stress:
1. Practice the Pause.
2. Count backwards from 10.
3. Take a deep breath in for the count of 3 hold for 3 release for 4 (equals 10).
4. Focus on inhaling positive vibes, holding them into your heart and then exhaling the negative junk that is not serving you.
5. Observe how you feel.

I mentioned breath work. So much data has come out in recent years on how just changing your breathing can have major improvements on your overall health. When we are overwhelmed or depressed our breath can be quite compromised. Focused breath can reduce stress and anxiety,calm the mind, increase in energy and relieve muscle tension. For instance, practicing nasal breathing can move your body away from your sympathetic or "fight or flight" nervous system and lead you to the use of your parasympathetic nervous system which will lead to calming the mind and body.

5. Be one with Nature

Getting outside and soaking in the fresh air, sunshine and the beauty is free and therapeutic for most people. This seems obvious to do but many get so stuck and down that the thought of changing our environment is just too overwhelming. Sometimes we must force ourselves to just pick up our body and plant it somewhere else. There is incredible beauty surrounding us on our planet and I believe God created all of it for us to enjoy and find peace within. I encourage you to plant a garden, take a hike, sit by the water, smell a flower or just sit under a tree.

One of my favorite fundraisers in memory of Steven was held by my brother Ron who is a high school science teacher as well as a nature guru. It was a 33-mile hike through the Pinelands Nature Preserve in Southern New Jersey. About 20 people gathered for an overnight camping trip and hike through the beautiful Batona trails of the Pinelands in the spring of 2005. Yes we raised money towards research, but more importantly we came together in nature to remember Steven and all those touched by this horrible disease. As I sat around the campfire that night and listened to the fiddle and guitar that my brother and Dad played, I couldn't help but feel at peace surrounded by so much love for my little boy resting in eternity, waiting for us to be reunited. I feel closest to loved ones gone before when I am in God's playground.

As I was looking through Steven's memory box (which holds items from his life as well as meaningful mementos that honor him) I came across this poem that was written by Ron for this hike:

Footsteps quiet
Perhaps unheard
Voices low
Not a word
Yet you are here
Beside me still
To walk this path
At least until
I arrive, a destination
To join with you, a celebration
I miss you so and seek your hand

To hold my heart
And understand
That with life's journey
Some move along
For elsewhere calls
By wind and song
And so some tomorrow, we unite
To grow our love in God's warm light.

Something else we did to memorialize Steven was to plant a special garden. We started this when we lived in Maryland. The initial tree we planted came with us for each move and now has grown so large in our backyard in Delaware.

This is my place to feel his presence. I truly believe he is with me but I feel him more outside. I look at the tree we planted. It started out as a little seedling and has grown into a tall full tree. I use this as a metaphor. Time has passed so quickly, yet feels like yesterday. The tree represents the growth of my soul and the sprouting of my purpose. Reflecting back nineteen plus years ago I can immediately see my grieving torn self and then I focus on how I have grown spiritually and emotionally through the years and I am incredibly proud of my journey.

6. Sleep

Until recently I underestimated the importance of sleep. So many people pride themselves on only getting a few hours of shuteye a night. Think about some nights you have only gotten a few hours of sleep. How do you feel and how efficient are you? When I have a bad broken night of sleep

I feel sick, I can't focus, I eat more and just don't feel good. For many years I have struggled with sleep. Sometimes I fear it because I know my mind will take me places I don't want to visit or I wake up after a few hours and struggle to get back to sleep. For several years after Steven passed I would load up on Benadryl as my daughter slept between me and my husband. I spent countless hours torturing myself with unpleasant thoughts and what if scenarios. I worried if I shut my eyes they may come to fruition. When you experience grief and stressful times, sleep can be extremely challenging. Check out this list of ill effects of too little sleep:

- Lack of focus/concentration
- Mood changes
- Can lead to weight gain
- Can lead to higher blood pressure
- Can lead to higher insulin levels
- More prone to accidents
- Weakened immunity
- Poor balance

So what can we do to help us get 7 to 8 hours of suggested shut eye? Start with implementing the following:

1.Eliminate blue light an hour before bedtime. This includes your phone, computer and tv.
2. Meditate/Pray-quiet and calm your mind by focusing on positive thoughts, deep breathing and listen to light music.
3. Hack your sleep environment. This includes your mattress,pillow,lighting and temperature of the room.
4. Avoid caffeine and alcohol late in the day.
5. Avoid snacking a couple hours before bedtime.
6.Stick to a schedule-go to bed at the same time each night and get up at same time each morning.

7. Feed your body the right fuel

I know this is not a nutrition/health book, but I feel obligated to touch on what you fuel your body with will have a direct correlation to how you feel and overall wellness. For many years I would nutritionally sabotage my body with diet drinks, sugar and the latest fads. I was thin but certainly not healthy by any means. During the traumatic times I would have no appetite. The lack of nutrition would spiral me to feel more fatigued mentally and physically, and lead to unnecessary weight loss.

Over the years, I have educated myself on what my body needs to be strong and healthy! If you keep it simple, it boils down to real whole foods, minimally processed and from the Earth. God has provided what we need to sustain ourselves, however, humans have taken it and added many unhealthy ingredients. I use the 80/20 rule to my diet. Meaning, I eat proteins, carbs, healthy fats, fruits and veggies 80% of the time, and the other 20% I indulge in what I enjoy. Think of your body as a car. Would you fill the engine with "fake" or dirty gas? Of course not because we want it to run efficiently! Just keep it simple, look at the ingredients (no more than 5), be able to pronounce what is in your food and monitor your sodium and sugar intake. Oh-and drink the darn water to stay properly hydrated!

8. Hack your environment

I have found by controlling my environment, including my physical environment, where I spend the most time, the people I surround myself with and what I subject myself to it through social media, news etc., I have more control over my life. I find myself more at peace when I declutter and simplify my life. Think about the places you spend most of your time. Is it cluttered, messy, disorganized? How does this make you feel? When our space is disheveled our life can be too. Spend time organizing and "hacking" your environment so it brings you peace, joy and comfort. Take a look at your social environment. Jim Rohn, author, and motivational speaker, says, "You are the average of the five people you spend the most time with." Reflect on who your five are. Evaluate whether these people lift you up, challenge you, help you to strive to be better? You have the choice of who you allow to influence your life. If those you identified do not add value to your life, it may be time to find a new group of people.

When I attended the Ziglar Legacy Training I was surrounded by thirteen people from around the country that were like minded. They were ALL there to become a better version of themselves. We all came from such different backgrounds, however we had one thing in common: we invested in ourselves to become better people so we can serve others. I only spent three days with my new best friends, however I left with a little piece of all of them in my heart and learned and grew from each of them.

Our environment includes the most prime real estate - the space between our two ears. Evaluate what you are allowing into your mind. I love this quote by Zig Ziglar: "Your input determines your outlook. Your outlook determines your outlook and your output determines your future."

What is your input? Where are you receiving your input from? Is it valid, true and serving you or is it tainiting your mind causing negative thoughts which lead to the same behavior? If I had continued down the path I was on after Steven passed I would not be where I am today. My mind was constantly focused on the negative, sabotaging thoughts. I had been through such a traumatic event when Steven passed that all I could focus on was the bad things that could happen. This went on for years and was consistently backed up by more loss and trying times. What you feed your mind determines your appetite says Tom Ziglar and for sure my brain food was toxic! The million dollar question therefore is how do you change your input? This is not easy but possible and achievable if you believe it! Just like bad habits form over time, so do replacing these habits with good habits including your mindset. I also suggest eliminating the things in your life that dull your thoughts or cause negative thoughts.

Music

This may strike some people as odd listed under self care but music can be therapy for your soul. Studies show that it can also lift your mood,ease depression,slow heart rate and improve concentration. How does music make you feel? Certain songs can bring us back to special moments in our life or create more energy just listening to the beats and the words.There are certain songs that bring me back to holding Steven such as "To Where You Are" by Josh Groban. These lyrics are so appropriate for how I feel:

Who can say for certain
Maybe you're still here
I feel you all around me
Your memories so clear
Deep in the stillness

I can hear you speak
You're still an inspiration
Can it be
That you are mine
Forever love
And you are watching over me from up above
Fly me up to where you are
Beyond the distant star
I wish upon tonight
To see you smile
If only for awhile to know you're there
A breath away's not far
To where you are
Are you gently sleeping
Here inside my dream
And isn't faith believing
All power can't be seen
As my heart holds you
Just one beat away
I cherish all you gave me everyday
'Cause you are mine
Forever love
Watching me from up above
And I believe
That angels breathe
And that love will live on and never leave
Fly me up
To where you are
Beyond the distant star
I wish upon tonight
To see you smile
If only for awhile
To know you're there
A breath away's not far

To where you are
I know you're there
A breath away's not far
To where you are

I also have a feel good playlist that I blast when I am having a tough day or just need to move. I encourage you to create a list of the songs that light up your soul and transport you to a state of calmness or happiness.

10. Believe in the signs. Have faith.

Do you have a sign from your loved one? Are there odd times or events that occur in your life when you wonder if there is "divine" intervention? Why not believe?

The day of Steven's funeral was a cold and rainy one. He is resting in Lewisburg, Pennsylvania because when he passed we had no idea where we would settle down. My husband's family had some relatives in a beautiful cemetery (I hate this word) on the top of a hill overlooking a valley. It literally is one of the most beautiful peaceful places I could ask for. Back to the signs. That day as we were going through a drive thru to get Isobel something to eat, a bunch of ladybugs landed on the car. This was so unusual

at this time of year with this type of weather. I am not kidding. A ladybug stayed on the car all day! Ever since March 6th, 2002, ladybugs have visited me at the times I needed it the most.

One particular time that comes to mind is after my mom suffered her stroke. I was at the hospital in Trenton, New Jersey with her and I truly did not know if she was going to survive. I was struggling terribly and needed fresh air. As I stood outside I asked God for a sign that everything would be okay. The next minute, I looked in front of me at a light pole and there he was, my little ladybug.

My eyes burst in tears of relief and gratitude knowing that no matter the outcome, it would all be alright. Faith also allows us to be bigger than our fears. Surrendering to God's plan takes courage and trust. However, when you let go, the world of possibilities will open up to you. Keep your eyes open, be willing to seek out the signs from your loved ones, and have faith!

Chapter 11

Leaving a Legacy

*"Legacy is intentionally preparing
those you love to grow through
life's most difficult challenges."*
- Tom Ziglar

How ironic that I feel blessed for all the goodness that grief and pain has brought to my life. This may sound unbelievable, but I truly believe that without the sadness and scars, I would not be the person I am today. The overwhelming losses in the past years have ultimately brought me to my purpose and created my ultimate legacy.

Today, I fulfill my calling of helping women that feel hopeless, overwrought with grief and just don't know how to take care of themselves. Over the years, my plan slowly started to reveal itself. Maybe this was God's intention after all. I never shied away from telling others of my journey however I was good at masking the pain. I became so hardened from all the traumas that I was able to hold conversations with grieving moms and keep myself together.

Only later would the tears flow when I got in the shower. My heart ached for the pain others were experiencing as going through this myself I understood. Many times women didn't want to tell me what was on their heart because they didn't feel like their pain was justified knowing that I had lost a child. But, I always validate that their pain is real because they are the ones living it. What may seem trivial to some is gigantic to others.

If there is one thing I have learned from grief it can mask in so many different ways and can stem from the smallest of disappointments or expectations. As I have mentioned before we must not compare our experiences to others because for each person whatever it is to them is real and significant! After all unless you literally have walked in their shoes you just don't know. We are all given special gifts and talents in life, that doesn't mean everyone will use them.

We all get stuck, stressed, and we self-sabotage our own true purpose in life. I believe we are all designed with an important calling on our lives. For many, that calling gets lost because of the hardships and difficulty of life. I have trained, facilitated, and coached women over the past years, assisting them in navigating their storms and finding the anchor in the harbor. In partnering with women, my exhortation is the same: This is your incredible journey and you need to find your happiness and purpose according to what fills your cup. Our purpose can illuminate from the most painful times in our lives.

Indeed, life often feels like it's not fair. However, we have the power to accept our past, control what we can and change those things we are not happy with. I love the quote by Mary Engelbreit, "Don't look back. You are not going that way." There is no benefit to dwelling on what has happened. The power of happiness truly lies deep within us and how we develop our future. Finding our purpose despite the pain we experience in our lives will ultimately lead to happiness. I believe a purpose filled life abounds when we embrace the raw emotions, experience true love and loss and can see the "Why" hidden in plain sight. I encourage you to just put one foot in front of the other and eventually you will go from crawling to walking to running to your purpose.

Yes, there are still tears that flow in the shower, but this space is also where I create my ideas, calm my thoughts, "cleanse" my body and mind of stress from the day and just breathe. I have invisible wounds and even though they have slowly healed, the scar will forever be etched in my heart and mind. Once grief strikes it may feel like a weight we are always carrying around. Some days it may feel much heavier and other days we barely recognize its presence. But, as my friend Larry said, "grief can also be beautiful." It helps define true happiness. We can not truly experience the joys in life if we don't travel through the sorrows as well.

As a reminder my mentor and friend Tom Ziglar says: "Legacy is intentionally preparing those you love to grow through life's most difficult challenges." Ask yourself how you want to be remembered by your loved ones when you are gone from this physical world. Personally, I want my children and those that mean the most to say I created a ripple effect of love and hope despite the extreme suffering I endured and the difficult challenges I faced. I want them to say through all of my tears, I was triumphant!

I asked my sons to write what they have observed over the years and these words reinforce that I will leave a beautiful legacy. There's no other way to put it, other than my mom is a superhero. The death of my brother Steven caused so much pain for her. What I have witnessed, is the fact that she has found peace with it. Although it still hurts us all everyday, she has brought joy to other people affected by SMA. She became the president of the Delaware and New Jersey chapter of CURE SMA, and has hosted many fundraising events and it has brought hope to many. She turned the worst thing possible into something beautiful. She has opened my eyes, in a way that many people have gotten to see. She showed me that beauty can come out of the dark. For that, I can only thank her. Steven will always be a part of all of our lives, and although it makes me sad, at least I get to say it's a beautiful sadness. My mother is a superhero, no other way to put it. -Blaise (17)

When my mom told me she wanted me to write about how Steven has affected me and our family I didn't know what I was going to write. I wasn't born when he passed so I didn't have any memories of what he was like. I've seen videos and pictures of him and I've heard stories about what he was like, but I never had an experience with him. I have also been educated by my parents on what he died from (SMA). So, with the information I have on Steven and his life, I now have to answer my mom's question - how has he affected my mom, the rest of my family, and me.

I think his passing has made my mom and dad better people and parents. They have been through loss and suffering, and can use that to help others and teach me and my siblings lessons and other things. I also think his passing has strengthened my parents' faith and connection to each other. My parents also might be a little more protective than other parents because of Steven, but I don't think that is necessarily a bad thing. My sibling might have a different opinion on this though. My mom's profession I believe, being a life coach, personal trainer, and speaker, is because of Steven's presence in her life. Because of Steven, she found a way to guide and help people through her job and I think one of the reasons she wants to do that is because she doesn't want people to have to go through the same thing she did. I also know Steven affected my parents by making them strong mentally.

When it comes to my brother and sister I think they are also different people than they would have been if Steven didn't pass. Starting with my sister, she was the only one out of the three of us that met him and lived with him. She probably doesn't remember him since she wasn't even three when he died, but you might have to hear her side of the story. I think she may still have some worry and anxiety when me and Blaise do certain things because her younger brother died. My sister is definitely stronger because of Steven too. One example I have of this is when I was running with my sister a few years ago. I wanted to give it up and walk because I was tired, but Isobel told me that when she was tired or wanted to give up she thought about what Steven had to go through and it helped her to keep running. That thought inspired me too and it still does. My brother is also the same way although he never met Steven. I think he has been able to use Steven to help him mentally during his races as well as in other situations.

To answer the last part of the question on how Steven has affected me I think I have to start with how he has made me try to be a better person. I try to be nicer to people because they may have lost someone close to them. As with every other member of my family, I think I am mentally stronger than I would be if Steven was still here. I feel like there are some things I have done before like finishing in races or just doing hard things that I can do because I think of my oldest brother. Whether I met Steven or not wouldn't have mattered in my mind. I am still strong because of it and I know Steven has been there to help me through it. To sum up how Steven has changed us all I would just say he has made us stronger mentally and maybe even some cases physically. -Jake (14)

I will leave you with this quote that I have over a cherished picture of Steven. "It is not the number of breaths we take, but the moments that take our breath away." We never know when our last breath will be so embrace every moment,be present with the people you are with and the place you are in. Live and love with purpose. Life as we know it,is fleeting and in a blink of an eye we will be reunited with the ones that have gone before us.

This poem was written by my Father in memory of Steven. These words offer comfort and hope that we will be reunited with those who have gone before us and be greeted with open eager arms.

On The Other Side of Orion

On the other side of Orion
Beyond the curtains
Of the never ending Universe
Constellations sparkle in the vast lake
    Below.
The moon and planets
Forever search
For positions unfound
Comets swiftly gliding unceasingly
With their tales in
    Tow.

He waits upon the silver beach
Runs along the wetted sand
By golden waters
Chasing winged sandbirds
Fleeing his eager
Reach.
He rides a gilded horse
Among other cherubs
Singing songs
He rides, he gallops
His giggle displays his
Passion.
Then he and his horse
Are swept by soft winds
From the east
To glide among the galaxies
Ever proud, forever joyful
In angelic
Fashion.
With no time a barrier
No need for blinking beacons
Passing myriads of heavenly bodies
He lands upon his
Star.
A meeting ground of sorts
Home away from home
A place for us to see
To hold our hopes and gaze
Afar.
Sooner than the march
Of time
Long before the earth's
Ending
We will stand before the gate

The curtain moves
      Aside.
He will run racing to greet
Our coming
Arms stretched open to embrace
And talk about the time that passed
Then take us
For
      A
            Ride
And
      The
         Ride
               Will
                   Never
                       end.

-Popsy Smith

I asked family and friends closest to me, to write a testimonial of their observation of how I (we) navigated through the grief and these were just a few.

"Your purpose has always been to remember Steven, support research to help in any way you can! You are an inspiration in motivation. You have grieved but always wanted to make a difference in everyone and anyone's life. Even though you grieve you continue to push forward and motivate others which is outstanding. You are there for anyone who needs it, even if you want to hide yourself."

- My best friend since the age of 7 • Melinda

"I think the biggest thing that helped you through losing Steven was Isobel and Jay. I remember you and I having conversations about how hard it was for you and you'd said if you didn't have Isobel, you probably wouldn't be here. I know you finding the support groups helped and your family and friends.

As far as what inspired you to start the chapter and health/wellness, was your love for Steven, never wanting another family to go through what you guys went through, then having Blaise and Jake. The chapter gave you a purpose to get up in the morning and keep Steven's memory alive and help other families fight to keep going and to give them hope of a cure. Heather and I could go on and on. I love you sweetie and am SO proud of you!"

- My closest friend from college • Heather Morison

"First of all, I want to say what an amazing person you are. You (and my brother) have been through so much. You've managed to work through the grief, keep your marriage and family together and have created a great business too. I think there are many things that have gone into your healing: your work with SMA was a large piece of it. You and Jason helping other families was very selfless. I think keeping yourselves busy with the countless fundraising and events have been great for all of you. You've found a place in a great community with a lot of special support with wonderful friends too. It's important to have support from friends to help you heal. Running and working out is another piece of your healing. It's a positive focus point and I think that moved you into your business. First with Zumba and personal training and then with the creation of The Ice House. You're always helping others. You're an inspiration, Jess."

- My sister in law • Tanya

"No one can truly be in the mind of another and know the moments they are struggling with grief and where they found that moment of acceptance and to take action. That is what I saw in you. At some point, I am not sure exactly when you took action. I saw that you took steps. You made healthy choices. You endured physical pain through marathons that could never match the emotional pain you have gone through. I have thought that your "mind over matter" attitude allowed you to connect with your son on a spiritual level during these times. You are setting examples to live a full life. You've connected with families of SMA and have served them. You continue to connect with people and support them in their own personal journeys through self-care, empowering them to ultimately find their purpose. You have found meaning through these connections in that every person you meet regardless of what they are going through can take the steps to live a full life. Sharing your talents is a gift."

- My sister in law • Lisa

"Faith, the support of many, and a will powered by God's promise and love 'fuels' Jess's ability to cope daily with the death of Steven. She chooses to live life, and help others through her business and personal contacts.

Steven's SMA type 1 diagnosis could have doomed Jess's life forever, However, she received the grace of strength and perseverance.

Her husband (our son) Jason supported each step needed to 'run toward the pain' of loss on a daily basis.

Therefore, together they accepted how to change the things they could. Love from her family, friends and help from hundreds of supporters to the cause of finding a cure for SMA and the willingness to embrace the best in each day, Jess took on the pain of loss.

Steven still lives today because his parents embrace the impact that a tragedy can have a positive outcome. Steven is thought of and spoken of frequently. His spirit lives on through love and the work of many individuals.

It is heartwarming that Steven's sister and brothers have learned who he was. They know their brother's memory is a result of their family's passion to aid others through their need and pain. Through their loss, Jess and Jason have become positive teachers to Isobel, Blaise, and Jake and all who meet them."

- Dad & Mom Moyer

"As a mom and grandma, it is difficult to see your child go through such pain and grief. I would do anything to make it better. One moment of one day changed a life forever Although 19 years have gone by, every day for Jessica is a memory of Steven's life that recalls all the emotions. She has developed resiliency and strength because of Steven's presence in her life. Although she could not change Steven's life, she felt it was her goal or purpose in life to help others that could change their lifestyle for better health.

The development of treatments for SMA brings both tears of sadness and joy. All the fundraisers and events we have done in Steven's memory have come to fruition. Stevens presence in Jessica's life has allowed us to be part of a treatment and cure for SMA."

- Mom Smith

Jessica Moyer is a heartfelt national speaker, life coach, and author. Her passion and purpose to help women live fully through embracing their health (mentally, physically, emotionally, and spiritually) has led her to open a boutique wellness studio in Delaware. In addition, she is the owner of Purposeful Life & Wellness Coaching to help people find hope through loss and grief.

As a certified Ziglar Legacy Coach, John Maxwell Coach/ Trainer and ACE Personal Trainer she has helped thousands of women transform their lives. In addition, she holds many wellness certifications. She graduated Magna Sum Laud from Gannon University with a dual major in Business and Sociology and minor in Personal Training.

Her passion to help her community is evident in her involvement in many different charities; President of Cure SMA Delaware/South Jersey Chapter, participant of Dancing with Delaware Stars to benefit Mom's house and Boys & Girls Club as well as supporter of many others. She also served as an honorary commander for three years at the Dover Air Force Base.

Most importantly she is devoted to her amazing husband Jason Moyer (O.D. and a Major in the Delaware Air National Guard) as well as a loving mother to four beautiful children, Isobel, Blaise, Jake and (angel Steven). She is passionate about her faith in God, running, fitness, community, and travel. Her soul calling is helping women identify, and live their purpose through a vibrant and healthy lifestyle!

For more info or to contact Jessica:

www.PurposefulLifeWellnessCoach.com
jessica@purposefullifewellnesscoach.com
302-233-3795
fb:Jessica Smith Moyer
IG: moyer.jessica

Enroll with Jessica for one-on-one life coaching sessions:

To schedule a complimentary coaching call:
(12 sessions)
http://calendly.com/purposefullifewellness/free-wellness-session

Book Jessica for Customized Speaking Engagements:

Self-care Through Grief & Loss
Living a Resilient Focused Life
Empowering Women to Live Their Most Incredible Life
Finding Your Purpose Through Your Pain

Personal Fitness Training with Jessica

If you are interested in ordering 50 or more copies, please contact New Vibe Press at 503-372-6101 or email us at admin@newvibetraining.com.

Acknowledgements:

My loving husband Jason and beautiful children
Isobel, Blaise, and Jake

Ann Marie Shea
Bookbound by the Sea/Michelle Prince
In memory of my cousin Kim DiPietro
JillMarie Wiles
Justine Nichols
Lisa Smith-Graphic Designer
My in-laws Steve and Pat Moyer
My parents-Joan and Michael Smith
New Vibe Press/Carl Casanova
Ron Smith
Shannon Ritter Photography
Stacey Lane Clendaniel
Tanya and Doug Drennen
Tom Ziglar-mentor
ZLC Class of 23

Jake, Blaise, Jessica, Jason and Isobel Moyer
photo credit: Greg Lehr Photography

Your Story is Our Story
Your Story is Our Story!

Made in the USA
Middletown, DE
29 July 2022